THE BEST OF
GHOSTS
CAUGHT ON FILM

THE PARANORMAL AND THE SUPERNATURAL CAUGHT ON CAMERA

THE BEST OF
GHOSTS
CAUGHT ON FILM

THE PARANORMAL AND THE SUPERNATURAL CAUGHT ON CAMERA

D&C
David and Charles

DR MELVYN WILLIN WITH JIM EATON

Contents

Introduction

Welcome to the world of the extremely weird. This used to be called the 'supernatural', but the implication that unexplained phenomena were *above* nature rather than *within* it caused some problems, so people now tend to call it the 'paranormal' or beside the normal. I'm not too keen on that term either, since I would like to think that at least some of the phenomena within its remit are not paranormal at all, and that once explained they will become normal. 'Parapsychology' and 'experimental psychology' are too narrow to describe much of what is here, and even 'psychical research' excludes some very interesting anomalies. So perhaps I should stay with 'extremely weird'!

This book examines many photographs of so-called ghosts and also investigates other paranormal phenomena that people believe they have captured on film. But what exactly are ghosts? Are they really the elusive appearance of a dead person? Or does the human mind have the power to somehow project apparitions into the physical sphere?

Perhaps they are a short-circuit in time, allowing us to glimpse the past; seeing a living person go about their business in their time, but appear as a ghost in ours. But ghosts are not necessarily visible, they may be spirits or the souls of the departed manifesting themselves as strange and unexplained lights, or in the activity of poltergeists randomly moving objects.

The problem, of course, is that the evidence is not conclusive. A photograph of a ghost is rarely claimed, although hauntings are relatively common. Strange noises, smells, changes in temperature and so on are often reported and some locations have won a considerable reputation for being haunted. However very few of the photographs in this book come from these places or from deliberate and planned

photographing in a location where there have been ghost sightings. There are some famous exceptions, but by and large the photographs in existence that seem to defy any natural explanation have occurred by chance.

Typically the photographer takes a routine photograph and later discovers that something strange had appeared on the film that was certainly not in frame when the shutter was pressed. When no obvious explanation seems to present itself, they seek the advice of experts (with many pictures in this book from the Society for Psychical Research). If the usual objections of multiple exposure, reflections and so on can be eliminated, then we are left with a mystery.

One could argue that the fact that the photographers had no special knowledge or interest in the paranormal means we should be a little less inclined to be sceptical about the circumstances of the pictures, there is no vested interest on their part as there might be with a ghost hunter or medium. But even if you can dismiss all but one of the photographs in this book as fake or mere coincidence, then that one is enough to allow the possibility that ghosts exist and may have been caught on film.

When I lecture in psychical research I always explain the basis for deciding what makes a photograph worth exhibiting and discussing. Not all of my chart of questions to establish veracity or mystery (next page) can be asked of every photograph, and only you will know the answers that are correct for you. Just as I find with my classes – and with me – the results are sometimes surprising. Yet every time you go through the process you will acquire a greater knowledge of your own strengths of belief and scepticism. That can only be a good thing. Here are some of the questions I ask:

- Is this photograph a deliberate fraud?
- Did an accidental flaw in photographic film or its development produce this image?
- Did the photographer knowingly use other people and/or props to achieve the images?

- Did the photographer forget or not notice other people in view at the time?
- Could the photograph be explained simply as the result of a repeatable or generally understood effect of light, or by an accidental intrusion in front of the lens?
- Does the photograph genuinely show an anomalous effect that is nonetheless within nature, but not currently understood?
- Does it genuinely show a paranormal effect that is outside nature as we understand it, and is thus beyond our comprehension?
- If I believe the photograph to illustrate something paranormal, does this strengthen my belief in religion, alien entities, or other psychical phenomena, or vice versa.
- Am I absolutely convinced that I have found the correct answer to the previous questions?

To those questions I should perhaps add the most obvious. What should a ghost look like? Sometimes you will be surprised to find a photograph published in this book which is accepted as being fraudulent. Such categorization will have been done well after it was first published. I show it to you because it illustrates what people thought was possible at the time. From its invention in the 19th century until well into the 20th century most people firmly believed the camera could not lie. They would have looked at these images quite differently from citizens of the 21st century, and it is educative for us to try to see them as they would.

Throughout this book I try not to provide didactic answers to the questions that are put forward. There are two reasons for this. One is that the subject is so complicated that it would be impossible in a book of this size to explore in great depth the issues that are raised here. The implications of the paranormal touch many different disciplines. The obvious examples are parapsychology, psychology, sociology and theology, but I would expand that list to include all

the so-called 'hard' sciences as well as the arts. The second reason is that I would not presume to tell anyone that I have the answers to all the imponderable questions that arise. One's knowledge grows according to one's experiences and learning. I used to be sceptical about poltergeists, for instance, but my attitude changed considerably when I witnessed an incident at first hand – and had it verified by another person present. It seems to me the height of arrogance to believe that at any time one has the answers to life's mysteries. In all realms of study new information sometimes confirms theories, sometimes expands them and sometimes destroys them. Let us all keep trying to unravel these enigmas.

This book is aimed at a wide audience. Some will find it somewhat 'heavy' at times and others will desire more depth and academic scrutiny. Hopefully everyone will find it thought-provoking and, whether it is used as a coffee-table adornment or the basis of further research, I trust that it will be enjoyed. Perhaps it will encourage you to explore your own photograph albums to see if you have any strange or inexplicable shots lurking there. Further to this, I do encourage you to arm yourself with a camera at all times – in these days of camera phones it is almost always possible to take a snapshot. The more photographic evidence we can acquire, the greater the database we will build up for finding those few elusive photographs of genuine paranormal phenomena.

Happy viewing and happy reading!

Dr. Melvyn Willin
Honorary Archivist
Society for Psychical Research, London

GHOSTLY FIGURES

So what is a ghost and what are its characteristics? The answer to the first question is 'I don't know', but there is sufficient evidence (I don't use the word 'proof') to suggest a very wide range of characteristics.

It can be transparent or opaque.
It can be solid or cloudy.
It can be unaware of our presence or make contact.
It can manifest through all of our senses except taste.
It can be recognizable or unknown.
It may or may not be time- and/or place-orientated.
It may or may not appear at times of crisis.
It can be human, animal or even take the form of a mode of transport.
It can soothe us or occasionally frighten us.

That list is far from being conclusive, but I think we might agree that there are many different types of ghosts, just as there are many different types of living human experience of them and perhaps this is a clue to their nature. It may be that a ghostly emanation of any kind requires human contact to act as a catalyst to its existence. The folklorist Eric Maple believed that if people ceased to believe in ghosts, ghosts would no longer be able to function. The power of belief has a considerable effect on one's whole being, as can be seen in medical trials using placebo drugs that sometimes work as well as the real thing. Is it beyond the bounds of possibility that a strong enough belief might be able to conjure up sufficient energy to create a tangible presence? In the 1920s Alexandra David-Neel certainly believed that she created a mind form (tulpa) that had a tangible existence, was seen by other people and was difficult to dispose of. There have been other similar claims with veridical evidence to oppose the allegation of hallucination. Furthermore perhaps we are bound to have difficulties in capturing on film what is by its very nature beyond an obvious definition or essence. We can photograph what electricity can do and we can hear what radio waves can provide, but their palpability can be discerned only through other agents. If ghosts are an unknown form of energy, then to learn more about them we need to record and study them without either the closed minds of some scientists or the gullibility and sensationalism of some spirit seekers and 'ghostbusters'.

In this chapter you will find many British examples, as one would expect from this most haunted island, as well as several instances from elsewhere. The settings vary from churches and graveyards to a mirror and even a kitchen sink! Some are inside, some outside. The provenance also varies: in some instances there is good evidence from contactable people; in others the information we have about the image is vague and the people long gone. The photographs have been taken using a wide range of equipment from old cameras to new digital apparatus, including the ever-present mobile phone. Where film has been used it varies from colour of a reasonable quality to old black and white. Despite the advancement in photographic techniques, transferring images from the original into book form can cause a certain loss of clarity. The publishers have firmly resisted any temptation to enhance the photos in this book and I can assure the reader that some of the originals are even more startling than the reproductions presented here. This was brought home to me in a very forthright way during a recent visit to Hungary, when I tracked down the original photograph of the Karácsond Virgin Mary vision (discussed in *Ghosts Caught on Film*) and was amazed at how clear it was.

I hope you enjoy this chapter and that you show the photos to your friends and family. Hopefully they will disagree with your interpretation – and mine – and provide further insights into what is happening in these intriguing shots. You could even try to reproduce some of the effects yourself, which does not necessarily mean that the ones shown here were produced in the same way. If you find yourself at any of the locations, make sure you have a camera with you. Who knows, your photographs may be included in the next book!

The Headless Woman

'Mike' writes of this shot taken by his father on a visit to Edinburgh Castle in around the 1980s: Mike's mother and sister can be seen sitting on a cannon. He reports that the print was found by chance when they were 'cleaning up the house' after his mother's death. In fact the figure is not necessarily headless – the transparent nature of her form makes it possible that her head is lost in the shadow of the stonework. There is a possibility that the image was caused by a double exposure – intentional or otherwise. Another suggestion might be that a person was standing in shot and then moved away during the exposure to leave a ghostly effect. However, the shape and perspective seem wrong for that explanation; neither does the figure resemble a chemical stain in processing or a lighting anomaly. The clothing does not seem to be consistent with what other people in the shot are wearing. The sleeves appear to be 'puffed' and the figure may be wearing a long white tail coat or a full-length dress. We are left with a mystery – but no hard evidence of a 'headless Victorian woman'.

'The clothing does not seem to be consistent with what the other people in the shot are wearing'

Reaper at the Waterfall

This atmospheric photograph was sent to the website ghoststudy.com. The picture was accompanied by this note:

I'm not the person who actually took this picture. It was sent to me by a friend. This photo was captured in West Java in Indonesia at the bottom of Mount Gede. The people in this photo are high school students who held a camp on that mountain.

Despite the site operator appealing for anyone to provide evidence for or against its authenticiy, nothing else is known about this picture. It was suggested, however, that the figure might be part of the mountain's rock formation, since the texture was similar.

The image of the 'grim reaper' is popular in folklore and in the minds of people through films and the media generally. If one cannot accept that such a character actually exists, then another possibility might suggest that a thought form is being created here, but why it would occur in this form and on this occasion baffles me.

'If one cannot accept that such a character actually exists, then another possibility might suggest that a thought form is being created here'

Face in the Pulpit

From the archives of the Society for Psychical Research comes this baffling photograph seeming to show a male human face coming out of the stone. It was taken by Donald G MacKenzie in May 1928 in a church on the Scottish island of Iona. He claimed the church was empty at the time and that nobody to whom he showed the photo seemed to recognize the mystery person. Assuming he was telling the truth, this precludes the possibility of an accidental double exposure, since in that case he would surely have remembered the other person when he saw the developed photo, even if he had not really registered his presence at the time. Although a photo taken before the days of computer technology is less likely than a more recent one to have been faked, the disadvantage with something taken 80 years ago is that the people involved are generally no longer available to help with further investigation!

'He claimed the church was empty at the time and that nobody to whom he showed the photo seemed to recognize the mystery person'

Skeleton in the Stones

Egremont Castle in Cumbria is in ruins and not occupied. On 28 September 1977 this photograph was taken using a Polaroid Swinger camera. What started life as a standard shot of the photographer's boyfriend changed dramatically when she noticed various strange impressions, especially the semblance of a figure to the left and behind the seated man. Is it a skeleton wearing an orange frock coat with a raised ghostly hand holding a wand of some sort or is it a curious rock formation? Tourist Information advises that Jefferson's history of Allerdale-above-Derwent (near this site) mentions that 'several skeletons have been found at various times', though we have no specific evidence to link that statement with this photograph.

The tradition of the skull or skeleton being frightening has a long heritage in many cultures. As far back as the second century the Greek essayist Plutarch wrote in *Moralia* of the skeleton being a reminder of mortality; even today the skull and crossbones are commonly recognized as the flag of pirates. The association with death has been maintained throughout all the arts up to and including contemporary times. In music one encounters the 'danse macabre' (for instance Saint-Saëns' version), inspired by the poem of Henri Cazalis, and Liszt's *Todentanz* or 'dance of death', inspired by Holbein's woodcuts. There are many examples in the film genre, notably in Walt Disney's *Fantasia*, the impressive skeleton warriors created by Ray Harryhausen in *Jason and the Argonauts* and much more recently in *Pirates of the Caribbean* starring Johnny Depp.

'she noticed ... the semblance of a figure to the left and behind the seated man'

Ghost in the Kitchen Sink

The details behind this curious photograph from 1992 are somewhat bizarre and involve places as far apart as Sheffield in Yorkshire and Tunisia in Africa. Researchers from the popular British television programme *Schofield's Quest* forwarded the picture and this accompanying letter to Maurice Grosse, an expert in photographic anomalies. He was equally puzzled by it:

My name is Walter Collins, aged 15. Please, please, please help me and my mum to solve this mystery. The photograph appeared in our holiday 'snaps' from a two week holiday in Tunisia in 1992. The film was used and taken out of the camera in Tunisia. The strange thing is that the picture is in our kitchen at home. Another spooky thing is that there are two negative images on the negative strips, but only one print. HELP! It cannot possibly be someone dressed up because the person would be standing in our sink! (The side would not take the weight!) It has puzzled us for two years! I hope you can help!

If the story told is true then this is a very strange image indeed. Perhaps a combination of faulty memory and a double exposure produced this shot, or perhaps there is something more mysterious happening.

'It cannot possibly be someone dressed up because the person would be standing in our sink!'

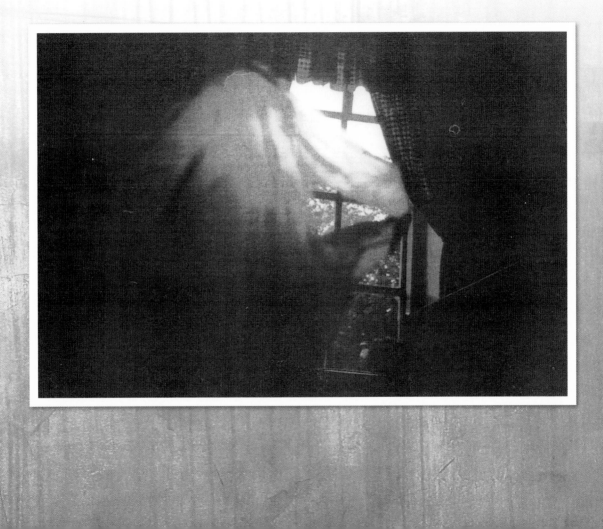

Extra Figure in the Fire Station

'there was nobody else in the station at that time, and this has been verified by all present'

We do not normally associate fire stations with paranormal phenomena and it therefore came as quite a surprise when Maurice Grosse was sent a complete set of photographs from the fire station at Market Deeping in Lincolnshire. Only the last shot showed the extra figure on the right inside the station doorway. The pictures were taken on 26 January 1986 from approximately 25m (80ft), with 5–6 second gaps between shots. Mr Adams of the fire service stated '…there was nobody else in the station at that time, and this has been verified by all present.'

I think one can discount either fraud, lighting effects or developing anomalies here, but the figure does appear to be very solid and I wonder whether it may be an extra person who accidentally came into view and whom the photographer had either forgotten about or not seen – photographer blindness. It might be an administrative worker, cleaner, friend or even a member of the public. The figure appears to be holding something in its right hand and wearing a white blouse or shirt – it has been suggested to me that it might have been a female worker with a handbag about to go off home. Despite interest from local and national television as well as the press, no reasonable answer has been found.

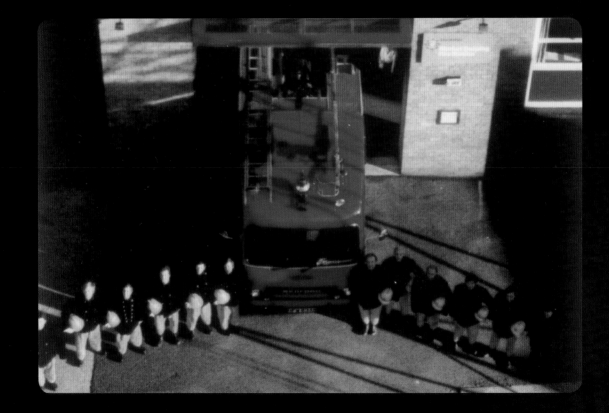

A Ghostly Prayer

The church in Eastry, near Sandwich in Kent, is dedicated to the Blessed Virgin Mary and is thought to date from the eleventh or twelfth century. The details for this photograph are scant. It is generally believed to have been taken by Mr Bootman (or Botman), a bank manager, in September 1956, when he was alone in the church except for a cleaning lady. Although the image is often referred to as a 'ghostly vicar' it is possible that lighting or the chemicals used in development 'created' the shadowy figure. This might then be an example of pareidolia; that is, twisting images around in one's mind to form a recognizable likeness. A double exposure would also produce a similar image.

Alan Murdie, ex-president of the Ghost Club, comments: 'I have come to the conclusion that apparitions cannot be photographed, although they might leave traces on film (fogs, smudges etc.) in the same way a fish may leave ripples on a pond – but the ripples are not the fish!' This viewpoint may be sceptical, but it still allows for the possibility of paranormal phenomena being caught on film. In this example, even if the image is not a ghost, a genuine unknown presence may still have caused the 'fogs, smudges etc.' to be manifested and photographed.

'the image is often referred to as a "ghostly vicar" '

Happy Hour, or the Witching Hour?

Some 15 years ago I held a number of investigations at the St Anne's Castle public house in Great Leighs, near Chelmsford, Essex. The pub has a long history of haunting and poltergeist activity, as well as a direct link to witchcraft via the story of the 'witch of Scrapfaggot Green' and the boulder that was placed over her grave and subsequently moved by American forces during the Second World War. On the occasion when this shot was taken I was with a group of experienced investigators who were placed at different locations in and around the pub with recording apparatus. Rules concerning the movement of people were strictly adhered to in order to avoid misunderstandings, and nobody was alone, since verification is always necessary for any subsequent claims.

Late into the night a muffled sound was heard and my companion Jeff took two quick shots into the darkness. We saw nothing except the flash of the camera illuminating the adjacent room. At the end of the stake-out we met up to discuss what had happened and confirmed that nobody had left their posts nor witnessed anything strange, apart from the usual coldness and excitement at the possibility of capturing something paranormal. It seemed that the investigation had been a failure until the two photos were developed. One showed the empty room and the other clearly showed an unknown woman seemingly dressed in modern clothes. It is possible that photographer (and observer) blindness was to blame, but the woman did not match the description of anyone else present. Of course, it could have been an intruder, but this also seems unlikely.

> 'Nobody had ... witnessed anything strange, apart from the usual coldness and excitement at the possibility of capturing something paranormal'

The Casino Ghost

'The shape seemed too clear to be dust or smoke'

This picture is one of many interesting images collected by the website ghoststudy.com and, unusually, it is accompanied by some details of its provenance. We are told that 'Mark' took the shot of his girlfriend with a camera phone at a restaurant at the Burswood Casino in Perth, Australia, on 16 February 2005. About a month later friends started pointing out the strange shape behind the girl's head. The shape seemed too clear to be dust or smoke and a double exposure on such a camera is very unlikely, if not impossible. It was suggested that the image could be that of a lady in an orange dress or something similar, with strangely coloured face and hair, but nobody seems to know for sure. Mark remains sceptical, but he is open-minded enough to admit that it is 'freaky'. Did someone pop in and out of the shot or is it an example of an apparition?

The photo is unusual in that paranormal images are not often taken in restaurants. We are all aware of the graveyard syndrome or haunted houses and castles, especially in the UK, but to capture such an image in this setting is particularly welcome. Perhaps it is another example of places holding 'highly charged' memories that can be conducive to paranormal phenomena.

Face in the Mirror

There seems nothing particularly unusual about this image at first glance. It is a room containing historic furniture – a four-poster bed, tapestry curtains. It is in fact a room in the Halls Croft Building in Stratford – the house that once belonged to Shakespeare's son-in-law and dates from the early seventeenth century. A member of the Haunted Britain investigative team was visiting the house and took this photograph, only later discovering the figure reflected in the mirror. According to the photographer, there was no one else in the room. If you imagine where the reflected person must have been standing, if indeed there had been someone there, he would have been just in front of the photographer to the left and facing him. Hard to miss, one would have thought! Could it be the apparition of one of the house's former inhabitants? The figure appears to have a dark jacket and white shirt or possibly a lace cravat – popular wear for gentlemen in the seventeenth century.

If there really was no one else present in the room, it is certainly intriguing, but I have in the past used mirrors to produce contrived shots that looked very convincing. At a 'ghost hunt' in Scarborough in the 1970s I was offered money by a newspaper to allow them to print my fake Polaroid of a reflected skull-like face as a genuine ghost photo. I declined their offer.

'the house ... once belonged to Shakespeare's son-in-law and dates from the early seventeenth century'

The Ghost of the *Mary Rose*

'There is no explanation for the white image that can be seen in the background'

This shot is both intriguing and frustrating. Dated 1995, it is part of the Maurice Grosse Collection held in the SPR Archive; although it is accompanied by a handwritten letter the details are inconclusive and the person named and the phone number given are no longer obtainable. What we do have is a photo 'taken from the Observation Gallery through a glass partition'. The person in shadow in the foreground would appear to be a lady carrying a bag over her left shoulder, standing in front of the exhibit of Henry VIII's flagship the *Mary Rose*. There is no explanation for the white image that can be seen in the background. Maurice Grosse obviously thought it worthy of further investigation, but his precise findings have not been discovered. The mystery remains.

STRANGE LIGHTS & APPARITIONS

'Strange lights and apparitions' – a title with two concepts and multiple interpretations, some separate and some entwined. The strange lights could be just that, which would have justified my including the aurora borealis (northern lights) or the light quality experienced during an eclipse. However, with the photos of lights shown here, there is an implication that something we don't understand is happening. That leads us into the possible world of the apparition – a notoriously loaded word and open to as many definitions as one can imagine. To cite just one example from this chapter, consider the photograph taken in Cyprus (see page 56): is it an apparition or simply a strange light? All the usual questions of verification and research can be asked of it, but one is still left with the same dilemma.

Within this chapter we also present a curious picture of what might be astral projection (see page 42). Sceptics will be horrified to read this, as may those who believe in the human soul, although the person photographed was not, as far as we know, having a near-death experience at the time. Do this and other light manifestations have a natural and simple explanation or are we discovering here something new and perhaps as controversial as an unknown energy field?

Probably the most contentious material in this chapter concerns the photographs of angels. The arguments attempting to refute the existence of angels are well known and I do not propose to go through them all here, but they include the fact that the wings of the stereotypical Renaissance angel are not big enough in relation to the body to enable lift-off unless the supernatural – yes, I mean 'supernatural' – is brought into play. Sceptics also maintain that angels are either figments of our imagination or semi-deities introduced in various mythologies, and notably in Christianity, to act as messengers to us and adversaries to those nasty demons. Let us not forget that Lucifer was himself a fallen angel. The idea of guardian angels was given a huge impetus after Arthur Machen's short story 'The Bowmen' – relating how the beleaguered British army was saved from possible annihilation when angelic bowmen appeared in the sky and drove away the enemy – was treated as fact after the Battle of Mons in Belgium on 23 August 1914. In the best possible tradition, of course, the angels were on the side of the good and righteous, which on this occasion would seem to mean the British. In the true spirit of urban legend what happened next was that people started coming forward, for whatever reasons – genuine, misguided or corrupt – to tell their personal experiences of what became known as the 'Angels of Mons'. The story spread and even became the subject for musical works such as Sydney Baldock's piano solo of the same name. According to the folklorist David Clarke on a far from final analysis, a researcher from the Imperial War Museum concluded: '… to pursue the supporting stories to source is to make a journey into a fog'.

We should, therefore, be very careful with the authenticity of the angel shots shown here. So why have I chosen to include them? The answer is partly, once again, that many, many people believe in such beings; and partly that they raise issues that are worthy of philosophical and moral discussion. If belief in a guardian angel allows a person to avoid taking responsibility for his or her own actions, should we then condone that belief? How do we know that the guardian angel isn't a deceiving demon or a helpful daemon?

If this is becoming somewhat mind-blowing, a return to relative – and it is only relative – normality might be achieved by perusing the image of the red doughnut on page 63: that surely can't be a manifestation of an angel!

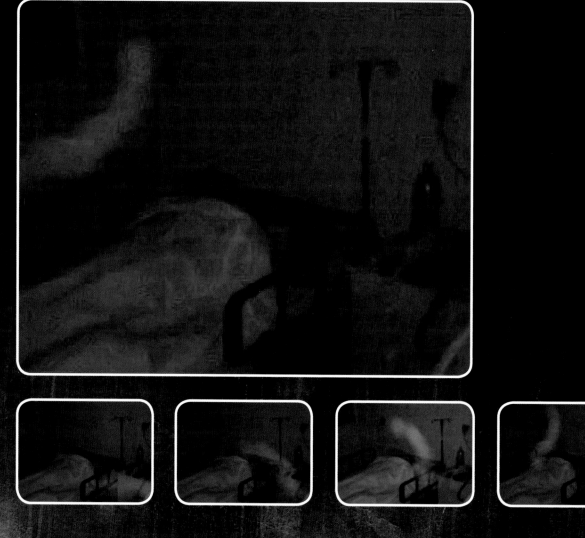

A Hovering Spirit

'Sceptics will advance natural causes such as dust pollution, condensation or lighting anomalies'

This very dark and indistinct photo was taken from a series of infrared digital video shots – five pictures from one second of video – recording a sleep-study session. These images are reminiscent of orbs, but with snake-like activity as opposed to ball movement with trails. There are many photos of orbs available, with varying degrees of clarity and information, and many different opinions about their origins. Sceptics will advance natural causes such as dust pollution, condensation or lighting anomalies, not to mention a deliberate fraud, but I once directed an investigation at the allegedly haunted Bell Hotel in Thetford, Norfolk, where we not only saw orbs with the naked eye but also filmed them in movement. Some religious adherents believe that a soul is revealing itself, others that an astral projection is occurring. Astral projection has been linked with modern studies of out-of-body experiences (OOBEs), notably by the late Arthur Ellison, a professor of electrical engineering, on the positive side and by the psychologist Dr Susan Blackmore from the sceptical viewpoint.

In these images, the effect seems to be moving in a non-random way as if it possessed some kind of will of its own, which may indicate something more than just an odd coincidence of lighting.

A Golden Angel

'he saw a luminous ball, photographed it and subsequently discovered this angelic form'

An intriguing picture about which we know very little. The only information I have managed to find is that a Swiss metal-bender called Silvio took this shot in 1978. Whether he was a metal-bender in the paranormal sense, like Uri Geller, or a hard-working sheet-metal worker, I do not know. Evidently Silvio's mother had recently died and whilst taking a walk in some unspecified woods he saw a luminous ball, photographed it and subsequently discovered this angelic form. It's another interesting light effect, but for me, despite the neat 'wings', the angel interpretation is less credible here. Its form seems rather more random or accidental than the Michigan Angel on page 53 but there is that same quality of incandescent light again. If it *is* faked, how and why did Silvio indulge in this subterfuge?

The Church Ghost

'The long exposure time would certainly produce an effect like this if someone had walked through the shot'

This shot was taken by Eddie Coxton on 12 September 1993 during a flower festival in a church in Staffordshire. Although he admits that there were other people in the church at the time he is adamant that no one was in front of the camera when he took this photograph on a 2–3 second exposure without flash. Questions: did he suffer from photographer's blindness and *did* someone briefly appear in the shot? The long exposure time would certainly produce an effect like this if someone had walked through the shot. Was the print damaged during development? Was the film faulty in the first place? Has the print been doctored to show an apparitional form? Or has Mr Coxton photographed a genuine ghost? Again we come back to the reliability of our information. It is easy to say that there is someone in the exposure. But if you were Mr Coxton and you *knew* there was no one there, what would you think then?

Copyright 1916 by
Dinklier & Blevins

Angel in the Sky

One Sandy Wasmer provides details of this old photograph on the website www.angelsghosts.com, informing us that:

I have a very old copy of this picture that was found in my grandfather's family bible when he died. Written on the back of the print was "1916 Arthur Hutchens – 4 Wells Kansas"…

Another website (tinet.org) claims it was taken in Oregon by a farmer called Dinklier J Blevins. The latter seems suspicious since the 'J' looks more like an ampersand to me. We are firmly in the realm of the 'Angels of Mons' (see page 39) here and many people will choose to interpret this cloud formation as a guardian angel fighting on the side of the great and the good. As I said in the introduction, if someone receives inspiration or comfort from this belief, there can surely be no objection to it, provided it does no one any harm.

A further explanation for the origin of such images might embrace 'thoughtography', whereby someone is actually imprinting on to the image a thought that is in their minds. This theory may sound bizarre, but is it any odder than the idea that there are angels fluttering around our skies?

'many people will choose to interpret this cloud formation as a guardian angel'

The Legend of the Haunted Cemetery

'There have often been stories of vampires associated with the area'

Highgate Cemetery in North London has a great deal of history and superstition attached to it. It was built in 1839 to relieve the overcrowded churchyards within the city and now covers 14 hectares (37 acres) of Grade Two listed parkland. There are 51,000 graves, with 850 classed as notable, including those of Karl Marx and Michael Faraday.

There have often been stories of vampires associated with the area. This photo was taken in November 1994 and nothing unusual was noticed at the time. However, on development, a strange, nebulous figure was noticed in the foreground. The negative was then sent to Maurice Grosse at the SPR, who was baffled. Is it possible that the effect was caused by chemical staining or even a defect in the original film or is it the appearance of something paranormal? It has not been possible to find the photographer – so if you know who it was, please get in touch!

Shimmering Angel

This image was sent to the website ghoststudy.com. It was evidently taken with a digital camera in Rockford, Michigan, and the person over whom the angel appears to be hovering was due to have surgery the next day. We are told that 'prayers were being said for a fast recovery' as the picture was taken.

The power of prayer has been commented on in many religious works and, indeed, I published an article myself comparing its veridical potential with that of spells undertaken by contemporary witches and Wiccans. Many people believe in the existence of guardian angels, be they discarnate (that is, disembodied) entities, religious manifestations or parts of their own psyche.

I discussed this image with a photographer and we agreed that there were two reasons to be suspicious about it: firstly, as with so many modern images, it could easily have been tampered with and the tampering, if done by an expert, would not be readily detectable; and secondly, the suggestion of a guardian angel shows a lack of objectivity. The photographer wondered why Scott, when submitting the photograph to the website, had not invited suggestions rather than dictating the image's angelic provenance. However, there is no denying the angelic form that the image takes, and the quality of the light is so strikingly similar to 'The Missing Husband' image on page 41 that perhaps there really was an angel watching over these people that day.

'the person over whom the angel appears to be hovering was due to have surgery the next day'

Mysterious Mist

Readers of *Ghosts Caught on Film* will be aware of some of the history and hauntings attached to this cemetery in Illinois, and over the years mysterious mists have also been filmed which people have claimed have not been attributable to weather conditions or breath being photographed accidentally. There have been a number of investigations, with different types of anomaly reported. Such mists are quite common either in conjunction with other paranormal events, as in the case of Belgrave Hall, Leicester (also discussed in *Ghosts Caught on Film*), or as a separate manifestation. These have included poltergeist activity (objects moving of their own accord) and alleged apparitions. A few years ago I attended a vigil at a derelict but allegedly haunted church in Essex and was able to video one such mist. I attributed this to the weather being conducive to such conditions, but a colleague believed it to be paranormal. Who is to say he was wrong and I was right or vice versa?

'mysterious mists have also been filmed which people have claimed have not been attributable to weather conditions'

The Cypriot Ghost

'he is adamant that nobody crossed in front of the wall where his camera was positioned'

George Kanigowski took this shot of the harbour lights at Limassol Bay on the night of 23 September 1986, when the temperature was about 29°C (84°F). He is able to be very particular about the circumstances of the shot (being taken on an Olympus OM10 camera on a tripod with 25 ASA Kodachrome film on a 30-second exposure without flash). He says he took five shots, each about two minutes apart, and he is adamant that nobody crossed in front of the wall where his camera was positioned. His girlfriend was with him at the time and verifies this. Although most of George's shots appeared normal after processing by Kodak back in England, one seems to contain an unknown effect. The lighting anomaly has a similar quality to the angel captured in St Peter's Basilica (see page 65) but that was apparently created by strong daylight – the source of this apparition is not so obvious.

A History of Pain

'one of the orphans
whose ghost is said
to roam the cloisters'

This intriguing image was taken by members of the Haunted Britain investigation team at the Royal Victoria Patriotic Building in South London. The eerie swirls of light look as if they may simply have been caused by the camera moving during the taking of the picture, but not only do the team claim that this was not the case, but the camera was actually mounted on a tripod at the time, and therefore incapable of movement.

The building itself has an intriguing past: built as an orphanage for daughters of servicemen who died in the Crimean War, it was nearly closed down following a scandal involving the abuse and death of one of the orphans whose ghost is said to roam the cloisters. During the First World War it was used as a military hospital; the field behind the building, now the cricket pitch, was filled with marquees housing as many as 1800 patients at any one time. During the Second World War the building became an alien clearing station run by MI6. It was rumoured that suspected spies were incarcerated for years, both in the building and in windowless concrete cells constructed in the south courtyard. So there's plenty of background for paranormal activity, but perhaps not enough to go on with these strange lights to speculate further.

The Virgin in Egypt

'If this was a
carefully planned
hoax one hopes
that it would have
been discovered and
the perpetrators
unmasked'

Visions of the Virgin Mary are numerous – Lourdes in France and Knock in Eire spring to mind – and she seems to appear in a number of guises, ranging from firm simulacra such as rocks and trees to water-based or aerial projections. We have photographic evidence for one of the more famous examples of the latter taken in 1968, showing what looks like a version of the Virgin Mary over the Coptic orthodox church of St Mary in Zeitoun, Egypt. The Virgin allegedly stayed there for some ten days and was seen by hundreds of people. If this was a carefully planned hoax one hopes that it would have been discovered and the perpetrators unmasked, but no such dénouement took place.

Mary appeared again in Cairo in 1986, coinciding with extensive power failures (not uncommon in Cairo at any time) and political upheavals. A sign from God; an elaborate hoax; a natural light/cloud formation? Again, it's for you to decide.

The Mysterious Red Doughnut

This is another of the many photographs of bizarre images that were sent to Maurice Grosse between 1977 and 2006. It was taken as a family shot of two children under perfectly normal circumstances in their garden in Stafford in 1994. Other photographs on the same film did not contain any unusual markings. However, the large red shape is quite unmistakable and almost seems to fit beneath the girl's arm. It has been suggested to me that the photographer's first finger and thumb might accidentally have been caught in the shot, but since cameras usually have the shutter button on the right hand side this would have made holding the camera very difficult. Furthermore, the colour would not seem to be appropriate. The 'camera strap' syndrome is often blamed for unaccountable shapes on the edge of photographs, but I don't think that works in this case. One commentator, perhaps with a degree of humour, suggested the image resembled a 'scrunchy' (a piece of elasticated material that holds long hair in place) that might have flown partially in front of the lens. With this example it has not been possible to view the negative to see if the red image is different there or to check for tampering.

'Other photographs on the same film did not contain any unusual markings'

Angel in the Vatican

'The blurred figure
may suggest an
angel'

This photo caused quite a storm when it appeared in the
Daily Express on 31 March 2007. It was taken by Andy Key,
a retired policeman, when he was visiting the Vatican and
listening to the Pope in St Peter's Basilica. Neither he nor
anyone else observed the figure and it was only when he and
his wife viewed the shots on his computer after returning
home that they noticed the anomaly. The blurred figure
may suggest an angel, but only in its traditional appearance
of a winged being, impregnated on our minds through
Renaissance artworks. Mr Key alleges that professional
photographers were baffled as to what caused it, but it seems
likely to be a coincidental play of light and reflections from
the window above. Mr Key also stressed that he and his wife
were not in Rome for religious reasons but simply sightseeing.
But the resemblance of the apparition to an angel greatly
adds to its power in a place of such religious significance.

SIMULACRA

My edition of *The Penguin English Dictionary* succinctly defines 'simulacrum' as a 'deceptive representation', but one needs to expand this here since the possibilities for finding simulacra are endless. One explanation suggests the concept of pareidolia, which the sceptic Robert Todd Carroll describes as:

A type of illusion or misperception involving a vague or obscure stimulus being perceived as something clear and distinct. For example, in the discolourations of a burnt tortilla one sees the face of Jesus Christ. Or one sees the image of Mother Teresa in a cinnamon bun, or the Virgin Mary in the bark of a tree.

From a vast store of possibilities I have included in this chapter examples of cloud formation, trees, rocks, wood, flower petals, glass reflections, concrete and even a baby scan. Religious imagery appears frequently, with the Virgin Mary and Jesus topping the bill, so to speak. As our brains try to make sense of our surroundings it is to be expected that we seek to translate everything we perceive into known images. There are anecdotal accounts of explorers' ships being invisible to the inhabitants of undiscovered shores as they approached, because the concept of a vast galleon was beyond the scope of the people's imaginations. There are many books devoted to the subject of optical illusions and we are all aware of the mirages caused by extreme weather conditions in the desert. A visit to an Imax 3D cinema will soon confirm our conditioning as we duck to avoid pterodactyls or spears thrown by enemy armies when our brains 'know' that it is just a flat screen in front of us. In our visually dominated society the ability to see and interpret is important to our well-being and ultimate survival, and we often believe the evidence of our eyes while neglecting our other senses. However, how often does our sight let us down by misinterpreting what we think we see?

So why devote a chapter to phenomena that are probably *not* paranormal? The simple answer is that many people believe that simulacra appear in order to convey a message either to an individual or to mankind as a whole. In a secular society it is easy to dismiss

religious representations as irrelevant, but if they affect vast numbers of people around the world then perhaps we should look more closely, if only to ask the question 'why'? Do the representations confirm or enhance people's beliefs; or does the naïveté of the believer discredit the belief itself? Such questions often lead to further questions and you might like to discuss the subject in more depth as you look at these images.

Of course, not all the photographs concern religious icons; a further Pandora's box could be opened about the famous 'face on Mars' image and the lesser-known statue-like figure – both shown in this chapter. I have a rather mischievous picture in my mind of space scientists tearing their hair out as the good and the great queue up to tell them these figures are not simply rock semblances of humans, but signs of life on Mars or evidence of earlier civilizations. The debate must point out that scientists have made some spectacular mistakes in the past and it would be so much more interesting if they were wrong on this occasion too!

What I find particularly enjoyable with these and other simulacra is the amount of discussion they generate. One starts with a photo and importantly says nothing about it, other than asking what it suggests to the viewer. What can follow is a number of different interpretations based on the beholders' levels of scepticism, religion, knowledge of the subject matter displayed and (I sincerely hope) sense of humour. I would encourage readers to start their own collections of such photos, since there is a great deal of material available all around us if we give our imaginations a chance.

Baby Scan or Baby Scam?

Ultrasound images of unborn babies like this will be familiar to parents everywhere, but this one comes with something extra. The scan is of Laurna Turner's unborn child, taken in Birmingham, England, in 2006 and appears to show the face of Jesus in the left centre. Finding such an image in a tree trunk or a stain on the wall is one thing, but imagine your feelings if the ultrasound scan of your baby appeared to show the image of Christ!

An eerie aside to this picture is that I found it in the archives of the agency Rex Features, the copy I saw bearing the word 'Rex' just above the image of Jesus ('rex' being the Latin word for 'king' and often applied to Jesus, for instance as in 'King of the Jews'). A simple coincidence but it gave me quite a shock nevertheless.

As far as I know, the story ends there. We can only assume that there was nothing unusual about the conception of Laurna's baby and I don't recall astronomers getting excited about any unusual activity in the night sky over Birmingham later that year.

'imagine your feelings if the ultrasound scan of your baby appeared to show the image of Christ!'

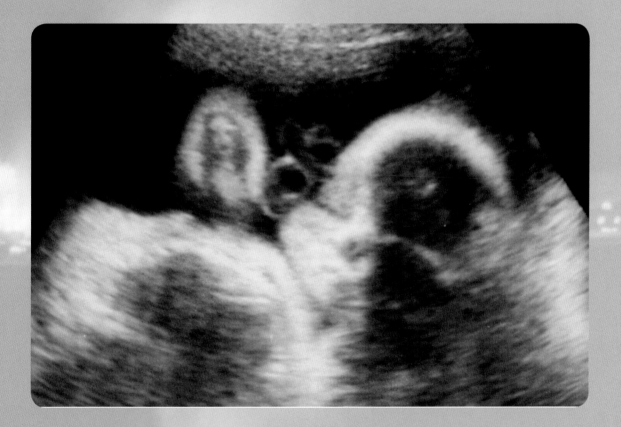

The Plate-Glass Virgin

The ever-popular Virgin Mary appeared yet again, this time in the glass of the Seminole Finance building in Clearwater, Florida, in November and December 1996. Although agnostics provided what they thought to be logical explanations for the image – namely water reflections or chemical deposits – this did not stop many people visiting the building and setting up shrines and vigils, believing that this was a sign from heaven. The incident subsequently received further publicity when nuns from the St Anne Order in Bangalore, India, confirmed its importance. When the weather and temperature changed, the vision disappeared from sight, presumably to reappear equally miraculously in another location. However you choose to interpret it, the image was thought-provoking enough for people to consider its message and decide on its authenticity accordingly.

'this did not stop many people visiting the building and setting up shrines and vigils'

71

Mars Mysteries

These controversial images are from the planet Mars. The first one was taken by the NASA spacecraft *Viking I* in 1976, in the region of Mars known as Cydonia and appears to show a face or mask; the other, taken by the Mars rover *Spirit* in 2004, appears to show a statue or a crouching figure.

With these images one is forced to choose between two conflicting interpretations. Richard Hoagland's *The Mars Mission* would have you believe that these structures were laid out by an alien civilization, that they convey a message to the inhabitants of Earth and that various sacred sites such as the Egyptian Sphinx and Avebury stone circle are connected to them in geometrical ways. A belief in conspiracy theories allows one to take the view that NASA may even agree with these revelations, but for political reasons is not allowed to disturb the world with its findings. A perhaps satirical (or worryingly perhaps not!) interpretation is offered by those claiming the second image to be a garden gnome, the Virgin Mary, Bigfoot or even a precursor of the Little Mermaid statue in Copenhagen. The opposing view, held by so-called 'hard' scientists, is that the formations are not manmade but are tricks of light and shadow; that they do not convey any sort of message and that they have been misinterpreted in line with the standard pareidolia principles of trying to find recognizable patterns in randomized configurations. The 'Man in the Moon' is a well-known example. You, the viewer, may wish to devise other possibilities.

'they convey a message to the inhabitants of Earth'

Madonna & Child Over the Rainbow

'An unknown friend later pointed out the anomaly in the sky'

Not possessing either original photographs or negatives is the bane of serious researchers of alleged photographic anomalies. This is one such example and is accordingly reliant upon indirect testimonies. One Ivy Wilson is said to have taken this shot of a rainbow at her home near Woombye, Queensland, Australia, in 1980. An unknown friend later pointed out the anomaly in the sky, suggesting that it could have been a reflection on glass from a statue in the house. Mrs Wilson maintained that the photograph was taken outside and that she owned no such statues.

By way of a sequel to this event, the seer Susanna d'Amore later maintained that she had been led to the place by the spirit of the stigmatic Padre Pio (see the chapter, 'The Unexplained: Poltergeists & Other Phenomena', page 94, for more on stigmatism): 'She claimed a close encounter with the Blessed Virgin Mary there, bought a few acres of land at the site, and built a small chapel. She discovered a small spring whose water was believed to have healing qualities, and busloads of pilgrims began to arrive, some of whom claimed to witness "the miracle of the sun".'

Tree Spirit

This bizarre photo was sent to the psychical investigator and professional photographer Cyril Permutt in the late 1970s and it is housed in the SPR Archive, together with many other intriguing photographs. There are different ways of interpreting the image according to one's belief system. As we have seen before, the sceptic will claim it is simply a double exposure or simulacrum, of which there are many examples to be found in gnarled tree trunks. However, some pagan religions allocate entities to all aspects of nature, specifically earth, air, fire and water. Furthermore, pantheistic beliefs credit trees with having their own 'souls' (for want of a better word), which may become visible at unknown times and in unknown circumstances. A believer in pagan elementals could therefore easily be persuaded that a tree spirit had been caught on film here. Just because such appearances are extremely rare, should we discount them all as unacceptable?

'pantheistic beliefs credit trees with having their own "souls" '

The Virgin of the Rose Petals

Yet another instance of the Virgin Mary and Jesus appearing in unusual guises, this time in 1948, when rose petals bearing their images evidently dropped from the sky at a Carmelite convent in Lipa City in the Philippines. A novice called Teresita Castillo was allegedly contacted by an apparition of the Virgin and various paranormal phenomena occurred. The formal church took exception to this and the convent was 'sealed'. However, in 1990 there was a new outbreak of religious fervour – a white luminous outline of a female in prayer began to appear on one of the leaves of a tall coconut tree. A year later, rose petals began to fall straight from the sky again and six children playing in the garden at the convent saw a statue come to life. If you find yourself in the Philippines you might like to check this out. The address is Shrine of Our Lady Mary, Mediatrix of All Grace, Torres St, Antipola, Lipa City, Batangas. Good luck!

'Teresita Castillo was allegedly contacted by an apparition of the Virgin and various paranormal phenomena occurred'

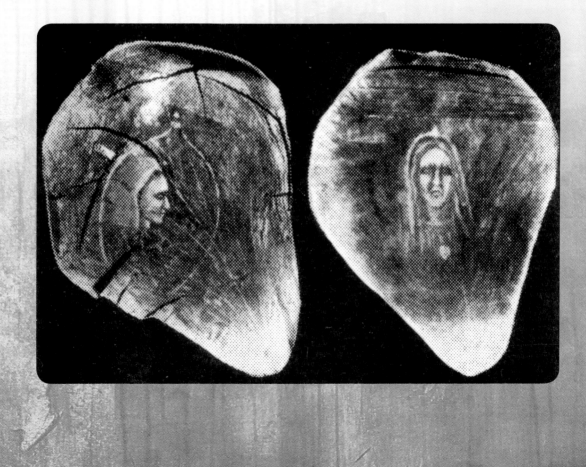

The Poplar Face

'one can ... indulge in some imaginative scenario involving a spirit of the woods'

This image was found in a plank of poplar wood from the mountains of West Virginia, USA, in October 1894. It is such an exceptionally clear representation of a hooded, bearded man that one wonders whether it has been doctored in some way either directly onto the wood or via the photo itself. Given the technical limitations of nineteenth-century photography, I think the latter unlikely, although the general public's ignorance of the photographic medium in its earlier days did lead to some fairly blatant, and what we would consider crude, hoaxes such as the Cottingley Fairies (see *Ghosts Caught on Film*). If, however, the face is genuine, then one can either accept it as a pleasant coincidence or indulge in some imaginative scenario involving a spirit of the woods leaving an imprint for all to see. It might, for instance, be argued that a local woodsman who either worked or died in the area manifested himself in this way as a reminder of his existence. But perhaps this stretches credulity too much.

The Face in the Cathedral

Images have appeared in stone for many years and when they have either resembled people associated with the place or have been so lifelike as to be undeniable faces – as for instance was the case at Belmez (see *Ghosts Caught on Film*) – they have been worthy of investigation. *Fortean Times* often prints such pictures, which have included such notables as Jesus Christ and Lady Diana – the latter in concrete, no less! The image here, from the same source, is from Christ Church Cathedral, Oxford, England, and purports to show Dean Liddell, the father of Lewis Carroll's Alice, who died in 1898. Furthermore, it is claimed that other faces also appeared near to that of the Dean. Damp walls often provide 'recognizable' images that the brain can process easily and once one has noticed a resemblance it is difficult to rid oneself of that interpretation. More positively, one might accept that these phenomena are genuine signs from unknown sources that appear now and then to extend our thought processes and beliefs.

'The image here ... purports to show Dean Liddell, the father of Lewis Carroll's Alice'

The Madonna of the Rocks

'It bears an extraordinary resemblance to traditional figures of the Madonna carrying the Christ-child'

'It bears an extraordinary resemblance to traditional figures of the Madonna carrying the Christ-child'

This rocky crag near Naples in Italy was photographed by Nick Yates of Brighouse in Yorkshire, England. It bears an extraordinary resemblance to traditional figures of the Madonna carrying the Christ-child, with Christ in this case apparently wearing a prominent crown, the 'crown' being the branches of a tree sprouting from the cliff. In fact it has been suggested that it actually looks more like the Virgin carrying a small stag than the baby Jesus, but this minor defect in an otherwise fascinating simulacrum is doubtless not enough to deter the faithful from seeing the divine in this work of nature.

Giant Ice Ghost

With simulacra we always need to maintain a balance between those that provoke serious thoughts and those that, however startling they may be, are open to a humorous interpretation. This picture is an obvious example of the latter; it was taken in Hocking Hills, Ohio, USA, and subsequently sent to the website ghoststudy.com. The comparative size of the figure in front of this ice formation indicates that the 'ghost' is quite a giant. It also looks just the way a fun ghost should look – one can almost hear it go 'boo'!

'It also looks just the way a fun ghost should look'

The Virgin in the Subway

'even in what many believe to be a secular society, religious beliefs and superstitions lurk just below the surface'

The date is 19 April 2005; the place is the Kennedy Expressway underpass, Chicago, Illinois, USA; the miracle is that a yellow and white stain on the concrete wall has formed itself into an image of the Virgin Mary on the day that Cardinal Joseph Ratzinger is elected Pope Benedict XVI. In reality the image was discovered the day before and then hysteria or curiosity took over, leading hundreds of people to visit the spot to leave flowers, candles and prayers. It is remarkable how demonstrative people become in response to this sort of occurrence. Perhaps it indicates that, even in what many believe to be a secular society, religious beliefs and superstitions lurk just below the surface.

Stains in concrete have appeared at various times as so-called paranormal phenomena: perhaps in some ways they have replaced the older 'significant' blood stains that couldn't be removed when a grisly crime had been committed. It is not my business to comment on people's belief systems; if they are happy to believe that Mary is contacting the world via a Chicago underpass then, if it does no harm to them or to others, so be it.

The Sleeping Woman

Some of the commonest and often most compelling simulacra are provided by the contours of trees and rocks. A good example is this 'sleeping woman' from Studley Royal Park in North Yorkshire, England, photographed by John Billingsley. Paranormal? Probably not, but one could argue that the tree produced this shape for a specific reason and that it was not a random growth, especially if the apparent image was meaningful to the viewer.

'one could argue that the tree produced this shape for a specific reason'

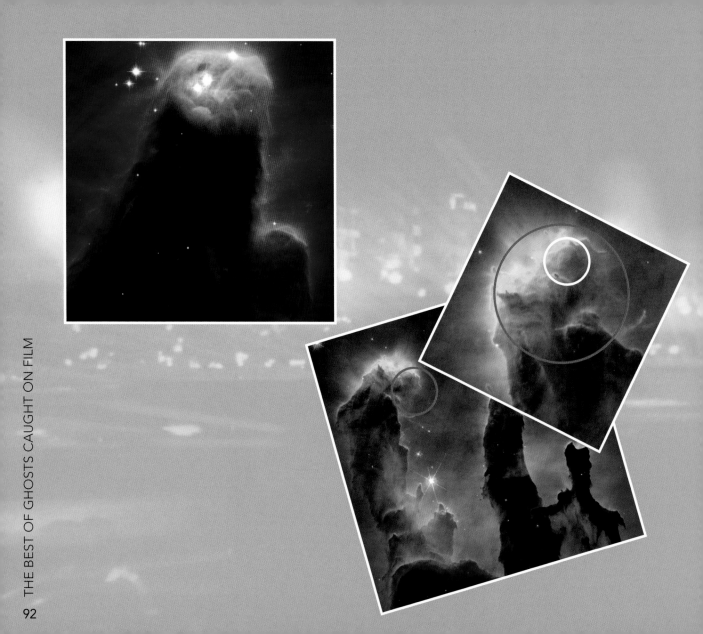

Images in the Heavens

The Hubble Space Telescope has revolutionized our view of the universe since it first started collecting data from the depths of the cosmos in 1990. It was perhaps inevitable that some people would look for and find divine meaning in these images and, sure enough, here are two examples of 'the face of Jesus' in deep space.

The first is the Cone Nebula – the lighter areas of gas cloud defining a mane of hair and shoulder, but the face, or where the face should be, is featureless darkness. In the Eagle Nebula the 'face' is more interesting. The towering pillars are formed from molecular hydrogen gas and dust and, rather fittingly, provide the conditions for the birth of new stars. At the peak of one of these pillars, once the image has been rotated 90 degrees, a recognizable face does appear on close inspection. What gets believers excited is this verse from the Gospel according to Matthew:

And then shall appear the sign of the Son of man in heaven: and then shall all the tribes of the earth mourn, and they shall see the Son of man coming in the clouds of heaven with power and great glory.

I am always one to advocate keeping an open mind, but on the other hand we should be careful not to remain so open-minded that our brains fall out!

'The towering pillars ... rather fittingly provide the conditions for the birth of new stars'

THE UNEXPLAINED: POLTERGEISTS & OTHER PHENOMENA

This is not quite a miscellaneous chapter, since a number of extremely interesting phenomena have been omitted. I hope that a future book may explore two very different worlds, namely those of the UFO and of cryptozoology, neither of which appears here. Instead we maintain a distinctly human emphasis, albeit in strange situations. The first is the phenomenon of the poltergeist, or noisy spirit. I have a particular interest here since I have witnessed poltergeist activity first hand and also had the privilege of undertaking a detailed study of the original documents and hundreds of hours of audio tape connected with the Enfield poltergeist (see page 97).

A return to occurrences connected with Christianity can be found in the examples of stigmata and alleged bleeding statues. The phenomenon of people displaying Christ's wounds is not new, but what makes it more interesting in the present day is the knowledge that forensic medical science can bring to the subject, as well as surveillance techniques to expose self-infliction. It seems possible, even likely, that in the relatively near future stigmatism will be understood as a psychosomatic condition, albeit a rare one, that can be treated, if desired, with surgery or drugs. Of course, some stigmatists consider themselves to be blessed rather than suffering, so they may well refuse medical help. The many hundreds of bleeding, oozing, weeping etc. statues from around the world can be investigated when permission is given. This can allow us to discover whether the emanations are unknown substances or melting paint, varnish, mineral deposits and the like occurring naturally or being introduced fraudulently to evoke greater belief in worshippers – and perhaps solicit donations.

The human body is a complicated organism and although we know far more about it now than we did even a few years ago, it would be ludicrous to suggest that our knowledge is complete. The mysterious auras that can be captured with specialist photography, with varying interpretations attached to the different colours, come into this category, as does the ominous predicament of spontaneous human combustion. There are several well-documented cases of the latter, and plenty of disagreement amongst experts as to whether it can happen and if so how. It would be interesting to ask a fireman for his views on whether a body can be reduced to ashes by a normal coal or wood fire, yet leave flammable objects and materials undamaged close by.

The final category in this chapter concerns our desire to fly or to defy gravity without pre-prepared environments or special equipment. Our society provides us with flying 'superheroes' like Superman and Batman; we also sometimes fly in our dreams and, if we believe the countless witnesses recorded in both folklore and history, some people do it by entering an altered state of consciousness. Flying has been a mixed blessing in the numerous examples recorded in church history, since angels and demons, saints and witches can all fly but have evoked somewhat different responses from the religions concerned. It would appear that some Buddhists and yogic practitioners can bounce higher than they should naturally be able to, and Spiritualism had its famous authenticated levitator in the person of Daniel Dunglas Home in nineteenth-century London. The Indian rope trick has been largely discredited and stage magicians have shown that they can reproduce virtually everything that can be achieved with alleged paranormal powers, but the fact that something can be replicated by conjuring skills does not mean that deception is employed every time it is done. Perhaps the people who genuinely possess these skills keep well away from the public eye to avoid the media attention and the constant testing in unnatural circumstances to which they would be submitted. If so, who can blame them?

The Enfield Poltergeist

The Enfield Poltergeist case was possibly the most thoroughly investigated paranormal event of the latter half of the twentieth century. The activities at a small house in Enfield, Middlesex, England, were extremely well documented over a period of more than a year around 1977 and have caused a great deal of controversy since. In this short space I can only give a tiny flavour of what happened: a serious researcher should read Playfair's *This House is Haunted* (1980) or examine the Maurice Grosse file which is part of the Society for Psychical Research Archives held at Cambridge University Library.

Briefly, inexplicable noises alerted the family to poltergeist activity that seemed to be particularly focused on one of the daughters, Janet, aged 11, and to a lesser extent her sister Margaret, who was 13. Neighbours, the police, journalists and finally psychical investigators were brought in to try to authenticate the events. This culminated in a large number of well-witnessed manifestations, including the movement of large pieces of furniture and other objects; Janet's levitation; the outbreak of inexplicable fires; and most spectacularly of all a gruff male voice – similar in some ways to Regan's voice in the film *The Exorcist* – coming from both girls.

To this day, on the rare occasions that Janet and Margaret are willing to talk about the events of 30 years ago, they maintain that the phenomena were genuine. I have personally spent a great deal of time both in conversation with the investigators and correlating the Enfield files for the SPR archive and I believe that at least some of the manifestations were real. Whether these photos of Janet levitating were part of that reality is for the viewer to decide.

'This culminated in a large number of well-witnessed manifestations'

Spontaneous Human Combustion

There has been much discussion and controversy concerning the existence of spontaneous human combustion (SHC) since Dickens mentioned it in *Bleak House*. A standard definition of this usually fatal condition is that the body seems to be consumed by fire without the involvement of an external agent. Often a part of the body, clothing or surrounding material is not burned. In some cases survivors have spoken of a fire seeming to come from within them and this has even been corroborated after medical examination. Experts in the nature and effects of fire have often disagreed and it is possible that some mysterious deaths by fire might be examples of SHC. Sceptics usually maintain that outside natural causes are to blame, which is strongly in opposition to the belief in psychosomatic suicide or some kind of demonic integration, whereby unknown occult practices cause the body to conflagrate in extreme circumstances currently beyond our understanding.

Numerous articles in publications such as the *Journal of the Society for Psychical Research*, *Fate Magazine* and *Fortean Times*, as well as the occasional television documentary, draw attention to SHC. Reported cases come from numerous countries and involve people from a variety of backgrounds. One well-known example was that of Dr John Thomas Bentley, who died in Pennsylvania, USA, in 1966. All that remained of him was a part of one lower leg with a foot and shoe intact.

The disturbing image reproduced here shows the aftermath of the death by fire of Ms E M, who was found in this state in London on 29 January 1958. She appears to have fallen into the fire, but the heat generated in an ordinary fire such as this would not be sufficient to reduce a body to ash. Other items close by, including a wooden chair and some textiles, do not seem to be affected. For a first-hand description of this phenomenon by John Heymer the interested reader should see *New Scientist*, 15 May 1986.

'when the victims have survived they have spoken of the fire seeming to come from within them

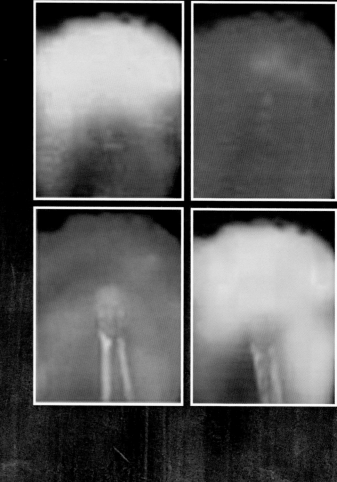

A Colourful Aura

The photographing of auras and the interpretation of the different colours still causes controversy and disagreement. My personal preference for purple was not manifested when I was photographed using this technique, since I was surrounded and to a large extent obliterated by the colour red. I was told it meant I had psychic abilities that I was blocking because of my 'sceptical nature'. The example presented here from Danièle Laurent provides quite a contrast to that shot of me, since a distinct image of the head and shoulders can be seen surrounded by purple and blue light. Different interpretors – or in some cases mediums – accord different meanings to different colours, which can indicate a range of aspects of the sitter's health and personality.

The photos were taken using a Polaroid camera while the subjects' fingers were resting on the electric 'plate' that allowed their auras to be manifested and captured on film. (Having been photographed this way myself, I can vouch for the fact that no pain is felt.) To obtain an auric photograph of yourself you might attend a Mind, Body, Spirit conference, where such things are often available.

'a distinct image of the head and shoulders can be seen surrounded by purple and blue light'

Yogic Flying

This is a practitioner of so-called 'yogic flying', a form of near-levitation carried out by followers of the Maharishi Mahesh Yogi and his form of Transcendental Meditation. There are various ways of interpreting what is happening here. A practitioner of yoga would argue that, as the mind and the body combine in an altered state of consciousness, the resulting lightness of spirit and body allows the body to bounce higher in the air than it would normally be able to do. Physical synchronicity is all-important both here and in the common party trick of lifting someone into the air using four people's fingertips, something I have done on many occasions. However, an opposing viewpoint might argue that the athleticism and flexibility of a fit and healthy human body could achieve this effect without the need for the yogic dimension. This photograph certainly makes the method look quite successful but the only moving film I have seen of the practice looks a lot more like hopping than flying. According to one practitioner it works like this:

People would rock gently, then more and more, and then start lifting off into the air. You should really be in a lotus position to do it – you can hurt yourself landing if you've got a dangling undercarriage. To begin with it's like the Wright brothers' first flight – you come down with a bump. That's why we have to sit on foam rubber cushions. Then you learn to control it better, and it becomes totally exhilarating.
(*Unexplained*, Volume 2, page 347, 1981)

'the resulting lightness of spirit and body allows the body to bounce higher in the air'

The Levitators

There are many examples of levitation from historical and folkloric sources and if just one of them is correct then we are left with a phenomenon that is not meant to exist … but does! The list of possible levitators includes such famous mediums as Daniel Dunglas Home and a bevy of saints including Joseph of Cupertino and Teresa of Avila. A stage magician – David Copperfield comes to mind here – might maintain that levitation is a trick and that with the correct devices and knowledge anyone can do it, whatever their state of mind. Perhaps psychology would emphasize the illusory nature of the phenomenon, suggesting that the body isn't really levitating but that the minds of both levitator and observer believe it is.

The two pictures shown here provide, at the very least, food for thought. In the first we see the Jesuit and investigator of the paranormal Father Quevedo performing levitation with a child: it may well be that he is demonstrating how easy it is to fool a gullible viewer. The other picture shows the Indian stage magician Yusultini and his wife Faeeza performing a levitation trick on a beach near Durban in South Africa. This photo has not been faked and there are none of the supporting wires or cables regularly assumed to be used in stage magic. Yusultini assures us that it is a trick, but he won't say how he does it!

'Yusultini assures us that it is a trick, but he won't say how he does it!'

Divine Blood & Tears

There is a huge choice available for readers who are interested in pursuing the phenomenon of weeping or bleeding statues of the Virgin Mary. *Fortean Times* is a good source of information on a range of examples, including the 'Weeping Virgin of Civitavecchia', the 'Weeping Virgin of Guadeloupe' and the 'Bleeding Madonna of Grangecon, County Wicklow'. The example chosen here, photographed on 20 March 2003, is generally known as the 'Weeping Virgin of Caracas, Venezuela'. Through an unpleasant coincidence the statue in San Cayetano Church started oozing in December 2002, a few days after a rally there where gunmen had killed three people, one of whom had been baptized in the church. The local priest, Father José Coromoto, reported that an invalid woman could walk freely after praying to the statue.

The crucifix pictured was photographed in the Vietnamese Catholic Church in Inala, Brisbane, Australia, on 27 May 2004 and allegedly shows Jesus weeping oil.

So what causes these exudations? One explanation, put forward by chemists, is that a hollow statue made out of porous matter can be filled with liquid, which will be sealed in after the outer shell has been glazed. If the glaze is then scratched, near the eyes for instance, the liquid will dribble out, resembling tear drops. Other possibilities are discoloured drips, perhaps from a ceiling, falling onto a statue or alterations in the statue's chemical composition due to changes in temperature. Plain fraud should not be overlooked, but neither should the beliefs of millions of Christians if a miraculous origin is to be suggested.

'The local priest ... reported that an invalid woman could walk freely after praying to the statue'

The Cottage Poltergeist

Ken Webster's book *The Vertical Plane* provides full details of this outbreak of poltergeist activity in 1984 at a cottage in Dodleston, Cheshire, England, during its renovation. The photos here, taken in May 1985, show what can happen to furniture when such an outbreak occurs. Mr Webster drew attention to a saucepan handle, shown in the shot, that later straightened itself. He also claimed to be receiving messages via paper that had previously been blank, chalk marks on the floor and even his computer. The originator was said to be one Tomas Harden, who lived in the cottage in the mid-sixteenth century.

The problem with these cases is one of belief. Do we believe that everything happened as documented or might it have been done fraudulently for any one of a number of reasons, including mischief, mental disease or financial gain? When the phenomenon has been witnessed by several different people independently it carries far more persuasion. As I mentioned earlier, I can assure the reader that my sceptical views about poltergeists changed dramatically once I had seen one in action.

'The originator was said to be one Tomas Harden, who lived in the cottage in the mid-sixteenth century'

The Stigmatist

In 1951 Antonio Ruffini beheld an apparition of the Virgin
Mary and received the wounds of Christ right the way through
his hands and feet. These photographs were taken in 1987 and
clearly show the scars more than 35 years later. Despite having
these wounds for many years Mr Ruffini's hands have not
become infected. He celebrated – if that is the right word – this
event by having a chapel built on the site of the apparition, to the
south of Rome.

There are many questions that might be posed here. Were
these wounds self-imposed either fully consciously or in some
altered, perhaps divine, state of consciousness? Might they have
appeared after deep meditation and then been maintained by
some gruesome self-infliction? It is well known that the body will
react physically to external psychological or emotional pressures
– blushing is a simple example. Many people will believe that
Mr Ruffini was indeed blessed by receiving these marks as a sign
from God and many stigmatists throughout the centuries have
displayed similar signs. The highly contentious and grisly issue of
Roman crucifixion techniques might also be considered: although
Renaissance paintings show Christ crucified with nails through his
hands and feet, it is often maintained that the nails would have to
be hammered through the wrists and heels in order to maintain
the body on a vertical plane… unless it was tied to the cross
first. But stigmatists do not display the wounds of Christ in these
places. This is indeed a difficult and disturbing subject.

'Many people will
believe that Mr
Ruffini was indeed
blessed by receiving
these marks as a sign
from God'

BACK FROM THE DEAD

I decided to exclude from this book the many possible spiritualistic photographs, some of which were displayed in *Ghosts Caught on Film*, since so many have later been discovered to be fraudulent. Instead, the title of this chapter implies the thorny issue of the survival of the spirit or soul after bodily death, an issue that is always hotly debated – and surely rightly so. The belief systems of various religions provide answers to this question and atheism deals with it easily by refusing to believe in it. But it remains a problem for the agnostics or 'don't knows' who must continue to thrash it around in their minds. I think it is useful to acquire as much evidence as possible in order to try to make sense of the issue. It must be comfortable to be convinced.

Therefore, depending on your point of view, the photographs in this final chapter will either challenge your religious beliefs, confirm your opinion of the gullibility of humans or continue to confuse and intrigue you. As in earlier chapters, frustratingly little information has been made available for some of the images, while others have covering letters detailing the circumstances in which they were taken. Often people have requested no publicity and wanted false names to be used in any filed documentation. In short they are worried that their friends or family will think them cranks or, in some cases, possessed. Photographs of this nature are sometimes sent to organizations like the Society for Psychical Research, many years after they were taken, because the strange appearances were not noticed on the initial superficial glance after development. A common approach is 'Please can you tell us what on earth that object/figure/face/blob/whatever is, since it was certainly not there when we took the photos.' In an ideal world the whole strip of negatives is enclosed: photographic experts can then scrutinize them for signs of tampering or other malfunctions.

My database from which I selected the contents of this final chapter has more interesting photos than any other section, far more than I have space to include. If one adds to these the photographic archives of the groups that have studied this work for, in some cases, well over a hundred years and then considers all the web pages devoted to the subject, there certainly seems to be evidence that something strange is going on here. After my previous book was published I received further information about some of the images in it, and I hope that this happens with this book too, especially concerning this chapter. I believe that we should all continue to explore this most important of undiscovered realms, namely what happens after physical death? Perhaps there is some evidence of tangible survival on the next few pages...

Grandfather Returns

This photograph was taken using a Polaroid camera in Magothy Beach, Maryland, USA, in 1985 – another of the interesting pictures posted on ghoststudy.com. The photographer explains:

We were taking a picture of my grandmother's house, and when the picture was taken… there was nobody in the picture. When the film started showing a picture, you could see an image of what appears to be a person walking up towards the house. My grandfather had just died about three months prior to this photo being taken… and in the photo the figure appears to be walking with his head bent down. This is how my grandfather would often walk.

For several reasons this is an interesting shot. Polaroid cameras do not have a negative and so it is difficult to tamper with pictures. There does appear to be someone in the shot, albeit somewhat blurred, and, according to one commentator, they seem not to be wearing any clothes. Very intriguing.

'My grandfather had just died about three months prior to this photo being taken'

Uninvited Wedding Guest

There are many images of this kind to be found on the internet and in magazines, and one must be very wary of the possibilities of reflection, paintings or people inside the buildings shown. This shot shows a father and daughter outside their house in Northern England, just before the daughter's wedding. Looking at it later she noticed an unknown face in the window – to the surprise of everyone who had been there, since there had been no one else either inside or outside the house at the time. They had the print tested and were told that it had not been tampered with in any way, but the negative was not available since the photographer could not be traced. According to a local writer the area had been used as an airfield during the Second World War and at one point had been bombed with a serious loss of life. Perhaps the face belonged to the ghost of a woman who had been killed then and was returning to the area, despite the fact that the house had been built 40 years after her death. Perhaps it was indeed a reflection from outside. Perhaps the missing negative was tampered with. We must decide for ourselves.

'there had been no one else either inside or outside the house at the time'

Highway Man

'could it just be a discolouration in the grass on the bank?'

Eric Spottke believes that the figure on the grass bank on the right of this road in Afton, Minnesota, USA, could be the ghost of a highway maintenance man killed in the area by a drunk driver. This would make it the scene of a violent or unnatural death which seems to accompany so many ghost stories. It certainly doesn't look like an innocent passer-by, the whitish blurred outline giving a definite other-worldly appearance to the figure, but could it just be a discolouration in the grass on the bank?

Roadside puzzles are more common than one might think and in England the phenomenon of hitchhikers who are picked up and subsequently vanish has been reported on many occasions. The area known as Blue Bell Hill in Kent was the scene of several mysterious appearances in 1992, when three different motorists at different times described what they believed to have been a motor accident involving a girl who had disappeared when they stopped their vehicles to help.

Graveyard Child

The story behind this photograph is tantalizing and frustratingly has little provenance other than reports on the website ghoststoriesandpictures.com. Despite its being a well-known and celebrated 'ghost photo', neither the identity of the graveyard nor that of the participants in the mystery are known. It appears that a 17-year-old Australian girl died in 1945 and her mother took this picture on a visit to her grave two years later. She was shocked to find that the photo included the image of a baby or child. She had no idea as to how she had managed to take such a picture or the identity of the child. As far as she could recall there hadn't been anyone else around the grave at the time. In 1990 a so-called 'paranormal expert' visited the area and found the graves of two babies next to the grave of the daughter. Without further details the story and picture have to remain anecdotal, but despite this it is not without points for discussion.

Double exposure is the most likely cause, although one would think that if such a simple explanation was likely, the photograph would never have achieved the notoriety it has. If the story is fraudulent then the only obvious explanation is that it was a somewhat distasteful prank. Death is difficult enough for most people to deal with, especially when a child is involved, so the appearance of the baby is a potent image that could lead to philosophizing on a number of matters embracing both religious and atheist viewpoints.

'the appearance of the baby is a potent image'

The Bruges Face

Researchers from the television programme *Schofield's Quest* forwarded a copy of this photograph to Maurice Grosse at the Society for Psychical Research after it had been sent to them with a request for clarification. The accompanying letter, dated 14 November 1994, was from a schoolgirl named Victoria from Grimsby in England, who wrote that her father had taken the picture on a school trip to Bruges in 1966. She provided considerable details and opinions as to its source, describing the face as that of a 'beaten-up boy' and the building as 'a gallery for the works of a Belgian artist, Hans Memling'. The photograph had appeared in the *Grimsby News* and had also been studied by the 'London Psychic Research' who asserted that is was a psychic phenomenon. According to the letter the building had been a convent in the thirteenth century and the nuns had found a beaten-up young boy on the steps of the building who they took in and cared for. The boy allegedly later became the celebrated artist Hans Memling.

There are a few problems with this information since Memling was born in Seligemstadt, Germany, between 1430 and 1440 and did not move to Bruges until about 1465 – he died there in 1494. Stories about his life do include his being injured at the Battle of Nancy in 1477 and being looked after by the Hospitallers of Bruges. The photograph could, of course, simply be a double exposure, and without further information it is difficult to form a definite opinion about its authenticity, particularly amid such a muddle of information. Nevertheless, if it is genuinely anomalous, it does seem quite impressive.

'the building had been a convent in the thirteenth century'

Rail Crash Ghost

This is another classic from the archive: a chilling photograph of a serious train crash in Scotland in 1937. Referred to at the time as the 'Castlecary Rail Disaster', it occurred between Glasgow and Edinburgh and was reported in the Glasgow *Daily Record*. The picture, which had accompanied the original report, was reissued in 1966 and appears to show a ghostly figure at one of the carriage doors. It is easy to dismiss it as a doll that has been propped up against the derailed train, but I think that idea needs questioning. Who would perpetrate a practical joke at the scene of such a disaster, especially considering that only the police, fire and ambulance services would have had access to the area? If the 'doll' was stood there to be identified by its owner at a later stage, why did this not happen after the photo was shown in the newspaper? What happened to the 'doll', which no one seems to have found after the area was cleared? Questions, questions with so few answers, which is all too common when one is investigating alleged paranormal phenomena.

'a ghostly figure at one of the carriage doors'

The Birthday Girl

This photograph was one of several taken on 24 June 1982 at a little girl's birthday party at her home in Coventry, Warwickshire, England. The photographer's father sent a letter of inquiry with further details:

When the developed film was collected it was found to have an additional image for which all reasonable explanations so far have eluded us. The garden is entirely fenced in by a six-foot fence with little or no chance of either dogs or intruders gaining entry without being observed.

The little girl seems to be aware of an elderly female figure whose face can be seen at the window. This could be a trick of the light showing some kind of reflection from inside, since the face is rather distorted. However, another photograph from the same film (in the Society for Psychical Research archives) does not show any such reflection. A medium who was given the photograph to 'read' for psychic phenomena felt there was a definite departed presence, 'unless Nanny was having a peep to see what she was doing'. Whether the face belongs to a living or dead relative is for the viewer to decide, but it seems unlikely that an unknown character managed to be photographed without anyone either realizing it or knowing who she was. It also seems unlikely that the family would bother to lie about the circumstances, since there was no prospect of either fame or financial reward. It remains a mystery.

'an elderly female figure whose face can be seen at the window'

Cabaret of the Departed

On 25 June 1992 the Society for Psychical Research received a letter from a Mrs G Webster of Halifax, West Yorkshire, England. She enclosed the photograph shown as well as its negative and a different photo of her parents, who had both died in the 1980s but were clearly the people in the background here. Mrs Webster wrote that the local chemist and photographic developer could not explain how they had appeared and that the strip of negatives showed the surrounding images to be normal. The photo was eventually sent to Dr Vernon Harrison, a past president of the Royal Photographic Society, who said that he did not think it was a double exposure and that the negative appeared to be 'normal'. He commented that the faces were about 1.7 times too big (presumably in comparison with everything else in the photograph) and that it did not seem probable that glass was being used to cause any reflections in the vicinity. Dr Harrison admitted that the effects could have been achieved using the process of photo-montage, but in this case it 'did not seem to be at all plausible'.

Maurice Grosse of the SPR believed that either the picture showed Mrs Webster's parents in apparitional form or a thought form had somehow been transferred onto the negative. He concluded, 'One thing is for certain, you have a remarkable photograph …' I agree with him.

'her parents ... had both died in the 1980s but were clearly the people in the background here'

The Grey Lady

'It has a tradition of being haunted by a person, usually referred to as a "grey lady"'

This picture was captured on the CCTV in the Reading Room of Willard Library, Evansville, Indiana, USA. It dates from July 2004 and is one of many sightings of the ghost caught on the library's webcam. The library is housed in a gothic building dating back to 1885. It has a tradition of being haunted by a person, usually referred to as a 'grey lady', who is seen briefly and then disappears without trace. The library actively promotes this image via its online video cameras, allowing the viewer to ghost-hunt from the comfort of his or her own home. As to the figure regularly spotted in the reading room there are, as always, various interpretations – a lighting anomaly, fraudulent activity or, of course, a ghost.

The Bogeywoman

This impressive photograph of a ghostly lady was taken in 1929 by Robert D Walsh at Fanham Wood Mill, USA, during the renovation of an inner staircase. She appears to be floating and looking towards the floor. Mr Walsh stated that he did not see anything unusual at the time and had taken the picture to help him assess how much timber would be needed for the building work. He did mention that his dog was acting 'different' that day, but did not specify what he meant by 'different'. The photograph came to light again more recently when it was put into the public domain by Mr Walsh's great-granddaughter. However, she related a story about being teased as a young girl by her sister with the threat that 'Sissy Breeze' would find her if she was naughty and said that Sissy was the person shown in the photograph. The addition of the sisters' childhood story of a 'bogeywoman' does not give any more concrete evidence to the photograph but it does add colour and the possibility that there was a tradition of hauntings at the site, or perhaps that the children were aware of a 'presence'.

'She appears to be floating and looking towards the floor'

Ghost of the Rail Crossing

Who or what is the ghostly figure on the left of this photograph? Is it a smudge in film processing or a phantom from beyond the grave? There are very few firm details concerning this allegedly haunted rail crossing in San Antonio, USA, and the spectral photograph taken by Andy and Debi Chesney. Most sources tell of a school bus stalling on the railway line and a train smashing into it and killing many of the passengers in the 1930s or 1940s. Unfortunately there appears to be no documentation of this tragedy; people seem to know of it only second-hand, as a ghost story. It has been reported that vehicles that stop near the train lines are pushed across the tracks to safety by unseen hands and furthermore that these hands belong to the spirits of the children killed there. Numerous tests have shown that vehicles do appear to roll over the tracks of their own volition and seemingly against the incline. This is not as unusual as one might expect: according to *Fortean Times* (December 2003), many other locations reproduce this anomaly. In tests where talcum powder has been sprinkled over vehicles to discover possible hand and finger prints, small, childlike prints have been produced. One particularly interested reporter, Brenda Pacheco, also heard children's voices and experienced droplets of blood materializing in her car at San Antonio. On the sceptical side, it has been claimed that, despite its appearance, the road has a downward incline towards the tracks and that the prints (from living children) could already have been on the vehicles concerned. Another possibility is that the horrendous bus crash that is known to have occurred in similar circumstances in Salt Lake City in 1938 may have been confused over the years and located in San Antonio by mistake.

'Numerous tests have shown that vehicles do appear to roll over the tracks of their own volition'

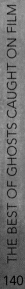

Figures in the Back Yard

What we are looking at here is not the bright point of light, which is the reflection of the photographic flash, but the figure to its left at the top of the garden. It was taken by an 80-year-old lady in Mount Juliet, Tennessee, who had apparently long claimed that there were ghosts who regularly visited her back yard. They would walk around for some time and then disappear. Not surprisingly she found that no one believed her and so she decided to take a photograph and prove it. Usually in such cases the photograph doesn't come out or the ghosts mysteriously stop visiting but, lo and behold, back they came and she took this picture. Her relative confirmed that it could not have been a reflection and that the old lady, who had difficulty walking, would hardly have been able to perpetrate such a hoax and she had no reason to do so anyway. The image was posted on the website ghoststudy.com by a researcher affiliated to the Alabama Foundation for Paranormal Research who claims to have visited the site and confirms that 'there really isn't anything that could have caused this by any explained reasoning'.

'there were ghosts who regularly visited her back yard'

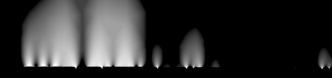

The early days of photography (in the later 19th century up to the early part of the 20th century) could be called 'The Golden Age of the Medium'. Many of the photographs from this era are now known to have been faked, but were so sincerely believed to have been genuine at the time that they are of interest to us here. It was an age when belief in the afterlife was almost universal, and an unexpected windfall from the new invention of photography was that it seemed to prove this. Plangent hope of a life hereafter was given to mourners when their nearest and dearest appeared to return from the grave to be photographed in their company. The semitransparent look of these spirits was blamed not on willfully deceptive double exposures, but on the insensitivity of camera film to the astral plane they inhabit when making earthly appearances. They were believed to mould themselves into their own likeness from profoundly mysterious ectoplasm, a vaporous substance, which supposedly emanated from the medium's body during a trance.

The most famous medium-photographers, such as Mumler (p.22), have generally been discredited but the legacy of their many surviving photographs demonstrates the widespread belief in this phenomenon across Europe and North America in the late 19th and early 20th centuries. Remember, at the time neither hypnotism nor photography was understood in the least by the general public. It was a time when almost everyone thought the camera could not lie. But it can. And now we would all accept that a crowd of onlookers who saw a person, animal, or bird emerge from what they were told was ectoplasm might well have been hypnotized, knowingly or not. Mass hypnotism is a fact, too.

Today we are less likely to accept the bird on Kluski's shoulder (p.20) is anything but real, of this world. The mystery to us is whether it was alive or dead, where it was before and where did it go after the séance? Some exponents might have been using rare forensic knowledge to exploit peculiarities of our eyes' behaviour. Remember, it is only because the eye retains an image for a split second that moving pictures and television were possible. Without knowing it we all have the facility to join up still pictures into a sense of movement, if they are shown to us quickly enough. What else, unsuspected by their audience, might one of these early performers have known and exploited, perhaps about the performance of light itself? In the middle of the 20th century the idea of laser lights, pencil thin as they race miles in a straight line, would have been laughed at. Today they are an unremarkable part of everyday life.

The people who supported these early mediums by lending their, sometimes august, names are quite as fascinating as the medium themselves. Sir William Crookes was one of the 19th century's most important scientists, doing work that led eventually to atomic theory. Was his life-long belief in the young medium Florence Cook based on the blind passion of an old fool for a young fool, or did he have to keep up his public face because it would have compromised his reputation as a scientist to admit he had quite literally been hoodwinked by cheap tricks? He could equally have been the only one who knew for sure her manifestations were genuine.

So, when you look at these remarkable photographs, look at them with two or three sets of eyes: eyes of the 19th, 20th, and 21st centuries. In the early 21st century few of us believe in fairies, and certainly not the winged dainties of the famous Cottingley photographs. Yet one hundred years ago most people thought that they just might be living at the bottom of someone's garden, maybe their own if only they knew how to see them.
Sir Arthur Conan Doyle, creator of Sherlock Holmes, definitely believed and detected nothing fake about the dancing fairies who had been enticed to dance for the camera. The best reason for explaining why he didn't see the clues to the fraud is because he didn't want to do so. This could well be why these photographs were accepted when they were first published, but are now regarded with more wariness. Look at all these photographs through 19th, 20th or 21st century eyes, and whatever you see, I know you will find them quite as absorbing as I always do.

Faker, Fakir or Floater?

LOCATION: The Conway Hall, London, England
DATE: 1937 or 1938

For two years Colin Evans had audiences believing they were seeing the sort of miracle they'd only read about in the Bible, or that they had heard the holy Hindu fakirs of India could do, almost at will. The ability to levitate has been documented throughout history. Saints with the gift include Teresa of Avila, Francis of Assisi, and the mystic Joseph of Cupertino, affectionately known as 'The Little Friar Who Flew'. As soon as cameras existed there were pictures of Indian fakirs seeming to defy gravity by extreme body control, or trickery. The Society for Psychical Research even possesses old film footage of this Indian Rope Trick, and recent commentators now believe they can explain why it was an illusion. Even in the 21st century such stage magicians as David Copperfield and David Blaine appear to levitate, but no one today quite believes what they are seeing.

'using spiritual powers to defy Earth's natural laws'

This infrared photograph of Colin Evans was not thought to be a trick or illusion, but a factual record of him floating 15 feet above the ground, usually for about a minute. Contemporary scrutiny of the photograph has not been so kind. Sceptics point out the creasing of his trousers could indicate a cord attached to him, and then threaded through the audience and attached to a pulley system behind the door at the back of the hall. There's definitely something suspicious seeming to hang from his left-hand side. But why did none of his audiences ever suspect or say he was playing a trick? There were two further possible answers. Either he was a master of mass hypnotism, or he really was using spiritual powers to defy Earth's natural laws.

Do you Believe in Fairies?

LOCATION: Cottingley Glen, near Bingley, West Yorkshire, England
DATE: July 1917

Perhaps the most charming and inspirational of all allegedly paranormal pictures, the dancing fairies of Cottingley Glen, were believed in for decades. In fact they were championed by Sir Arthur Conan Doyle, creator of Sherlock Holmes and noted devotee of deductive logic. He embraced Spiritualism and, curiously, both his father and grandfather used to draw fairies as a pastime, so they were nothing new to him.

'an impressive recorded example of the paranormal'

In 1917 Elsie Wright, 15, and her cousin Frances Griffiths, 10, showed off a set of photographs of winged fairies they had enticed to dance for them. Doyle and the fairy 'expert' Edward L. Gardner were convinced by them but Sir Oliver Lodge of the Society for Psychical Research suspected fraud. Yet, thanks to Doyle's 1922 book, *The Coming of the Fairies*, the Cottingley Fairies became firmly lodged as an impressive recorded example of the paranormal. What they hadn't remembered was *Princess Mary's Gift Book* of 1915. In 1977 the writer Fred Gettings recognized the Cottingley Fairies were the same as those in that book. Elsie and Frances were interviewed by researcher Joe Cooper and finally admitted their sixty-year trickery. Frances told the truth in *The Times*, March 18, 1977. Between 1982 and 1983 the *British Journal of Photography* published articles revealing the cut-outs had been held in place by hat pins, which close scrutiny should have observed. Then, in 1995, the conjurer James Randi pointed out the small waterfall behind the fairies was considerably blurred because of the exposure time, but the fairies' supposedly fluttering wings were in sharp focus. Yet none of these revelations have stopped some people still believing in fairies, as you probably know yourself.

Suspicious Spirit Séance

LOCATION: Mornington Road, London, England
DATE: May 1874

When this very famous photograph of a spirit manifestation was taken, the medium Florence Cook was seated to the right of the room. Cook's spirit form was known as Katie King, and the highly respected scientist and psychic investigator Sir William Crookes took 44 shots of her over three years, after which Katie King disappeared from Cook's séances. The speculation about Florence and her spirit manifestations is rich with juicy gossip and suspicion. She was only 18 in 1874 but Crookes was 42, and was suspected of enjoying a clandestine affair with the teenager. It can be argued Crookes publicly believed in Florence Cook's abilities as a medium only because he dared not compromise his enviable scientific reputation by admitting he was wrong. He was independently wealthy, and one of the most important scientists of the 19th century, in both the fields of physics and chemistry. He had discovered thallium in 1861 and his study of cathode rays laid the ground for atomic physics, so only the most rigid uprightness was attributed to him.

Reports about the Katie King séances are muddled, and there are even inconsistencies in Crookes' reports. Yet he attested to her reality for the rest of his life, saying to The British Association in 1898: 'outside our scientific knowledge there exists a Force exercised by intelligence differing from the ordinary intelligence common to mortals'. But did Crookes actually know that the medium Florence and her spirit Katie were the same person? There were plenty of clues this might have been so. When Sir George Sitwell once seized an apparent spirit manifestation, he found it was Florence herself, in her underwear.

'it was Florence herself, in her underwear'

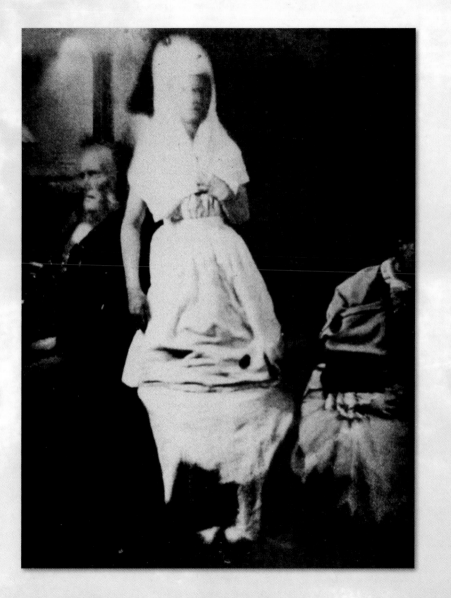

Eagle from the Ectoplasm

LOCATION: Unknown
DATE: 1919

Teofil Modrzejewski had a special claim among the mediums who produced physical phenomena from apparently empty air. He materialized dogs, cats, squirrels, a lion, and, on one auspicious occasion, a primordial man, part human and part ape. Born in Warsaw, Poland, in 1874, he worked as a bank manager and held séances under the pseudonym of Franek Kluski. He came to prominence after 1918 and also differed from other mediums by sometimes performing in a well-lit environment. This photograph was taken at a séance where, 'From the writhing mass of ectoplasm came a whirring and a rustling, then a beating of huge wings. Slowly there emerged a magnificent eagle…' (Barbanell: *The Newsletter*, Noah's Ark Society, September 1994.)

Not surprisingly, there has been considerable controversy concerning the authenticity of this and other phenomena Kluski produced. Consider the bird's size and short beak. These show it's not an eagle but some sort of hawk, something rather easier to conceal and reveal, and Barbanell doesn't explain how the slow cameras of the day managed to take such a sharp picture of the 'beating of huge wings'. The *Journal of the Society for Psychical Research* has featured articles arguing both for and against the authenticity of the photograph, as well as correspondence that continued well into the late 20th century. If the Kluski phenomena were not genuine then at the very least he was a brilliant conjurer and perhaps a mass hypnotist, too. This image retains considerable power and stimulates earnest discussion about the possibility of it being one of very few photographs ever to have been taken of an allegedly materialized bird.

'From the writhing mass of ectoplasm came a whirring and a rustling'

153

The Ghost of Abraham Lincoln

LOCATION: Studio in New York City, USA
DATE: 1869?

Spirit photographer William H. Mumler didn't know his sitter had lied. She said her name was Mrs. Tundall, and arrived in his studio in a black dress, bonnet and veil. In fact she was Mary Todd Lincoln, the murdered President's widow, something Mumler possibly didn't discover until the photograph he took was developed, clearly showing her dead husband with his hands resting on her shoulders.

‘the photograph clearly showed her dead husband with his hands resting on her shoulders’

Mumler is widely credited with discovering spirit photography – inventing it some would say. Originally an amateur photographer who worked engraving jewels in Boston, he was developing self-portraits when he noticed on one plate the extra figure of his cousin, who had died 12 years earlier. He almost immediately became celebrated as a photographer of departed spirits and was so successful he started taking such pictures full time. He then moved to New York, where his work gained much adulation. Other experts tested his methods, but they could not find fraud, and his fame spread to England. His book *Personal Experiences of William H. Mumler in Spirit Photography* is very illuminating about his methods, beliefs, and sitters. Some time around 1872, a young Master Herrod of North Bridgewood, Massachusetts, went into a trance and was photographed with the spirits of Europe, Asia, and America, and there are albums of mothers, fiancées, actresses, and spirit guides all hovering behind the pictures' living subjects. The only thing Mumler didn't see was his downfall, precipitated when it was discovered many of his wraiths were living people. He was acquitted of fraud after a court case, but never recovered and died in poverty in 1884.

The Posing Spirits

LOCATION: Frederick Hudson's studio, London, England
DATE: c.1875

This is attributed to the famous English spirit photographer, Frederick Hudson, whose pioneering studio was at 117 Holloway Road, London. It's said to be an image of his friend Mr. Raby, allegedly with the spirits of The Countess, James Lombard, Tommy, and of Mr. Wootton's mother. Hudson is supposed not to have touched the camera or the film, which was developed by others, as explained in an inscription: 'Obtained by Messrs. Raby, Wootton & Rutherford at Hudson's Studio. At a Séance at Mr. Wootton's the spirits desired him to go to Hudson's promising they would try to produce their likeness. Mr. W. did so, accompanied by his friends. The gentlemen operated themselves without allowing Hudson to take any part in the manipulations.'

'could not come up with logical explanations for the abnormal images'

But his friends did nothing to protect the plate from later tampering. Masking and 'Farmer's reducer' could all have been used to remove signs of deception. The editor of the *British Journal of Photography* investigated Hudson's studio the following year (bringing his own plates and chemicals) and could not come up with logical explanations for the abnormal images he also found. If the editor used Hudson's own camera then perhaps there is an explanation. Hudson is alleged to have had a specially adapted Howell camera, which contained a hidden metal frame that could be loaded with transparent waxed paper on to which the required ghostly image could be created. It clicked into place while the plate was exposed, adding its image, and then fell back into its hiding place. But this can't explain how some subjects were given recognizable pictures of dead sons and mothers. Although known to dress up and pose as his own 'ghosts' and to use double exposure for cheating, Hudson was ultimately believed to have leavened his frauds with much genuine spirit photography.

Phantoms in the Basilica

LOCATION: Basilica of Le Bois-Chenu, Domremy, France
DATE: 1925

The powerful provenance of this photograph is vital. It was taken in a much-revered basilica dedicated to St. Joan of Arc. St. Joan's history-changing spiritual experiences, allowing her to recognize an heir to the French throne she had never met and then to lead France to great battle victory, took place in woods close to this basilica. Lady Palmer took the photograph of her friend Miss Townsend and convincingly said no one else was in the basilica. But when the photograph was developed two figures dressed as priests appeared in the image.

> 'there is scarcely a place more likely in all of France for paranormal happenings'

The age of the photograph and the lack of any other evidence makes judging its veracity a problem. Undoubtedly, both women were aware of the great spiritual associations of the place. The heightened emotion caused by such a mystical setting is often associated with thoughtography. This is where the mind of the subject or the person behind the camera makes images appear spontaneously on film. In the case of this photograph, I think the idea of amateur double-exposure can be dismissed as something done consciously. But cameras of the time were hardly reliable and so an involuntary double exposure is always a possibility. Yet there is scarcely a place more likely in all of France for paranormal happenings. What do you think?

The Ghostly Peer in the Library

LOCATION: The library, Combermere Abbey, near Whitchurch, Cheshire, England
DATE: December 5, 1891

The inhabited remains of the 12th-century Benedictine abbey were especially still. Almost everyone was attending the funeral of Lord Combermere, who had been tragically killed in a horse and carriage accident. Miss Sybell Corbet took the opportunity to photograph his lordship's favourite chair in the library and swears neither of the two remaining staff entered that room during the one-hour exposure. She developed the plate herself and then discovered the undersized ghostly image of the dead peer, back in his favourite chair.

> 'and then discovered the undersized ghostly image of the dead peer, back in his favorite chair'

Sir William Barrett, a leading light in the Society for Psychical Research, originally thought the image was inconclusive, agreeing with others that one of the servants might have forgotten they went into the library. He changed his mind when Lord Combermere's daughter-in-law wrote to say none of the servants resembled the person photographed, and that all his lordship's children were convinced it was him, as reported in the *Journal of the Society for Psychical Research*, December 1895. There remain several problems to resolve if it is to be believed as a genuine ghostly image. For instance, the lord appears not to have any legs and some think his head is not in proportion to the ghostly arm. It is a real mystery but I still feel there could be an alternative non-paranormal explanation. Perhaps there was a lighting anomaly, but more likely a double exposure perpetrated by someone with a sense of humour.

PHOTOGRAPHING THE INVISIBLE

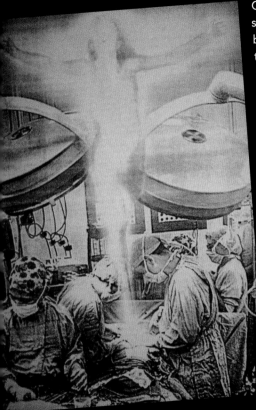

Can we photograph thoughts, the very pictures in our minds? Are there such things as auras, orbs or poltergeists? The notion that thoughts can be transferred directly onto photographic film is generally known as thoughtography. It seems untenable until you look at what Ted Serios produced between 1964 and 1967. The University of Maryland, Baltimore, has a very fine collection of well documented files and photographs produced by Serios which convinced psychic researcher Julie Eisenbud.
It seems foolhardy to believe every shot they took was fraudulent, especially because Eisenbud, and other witnesses, often changed the circumstances in which the photographs were taken.

Then, there is the idea that every living thing, including plants, has an aura, and this is something that appears to be demonstrable. Kirlian photography and human aura photography produce images that do what they claim – they record on film that which we do not normally see. The dispute lies in the source of these normally invisible manifestations, and what they can be taken to mean. The fact that bodies emit heat and that all organisms have an effect on their surroundings cannot be denied, but Kirlian photographs take this further, seeming to be able to produce phantom images of parts of, say, a leaf, still attached to the original but actually after it has been physically removed. No special meanings have been attached to such photographs, unlike those of humans.
The interpretation of people's health and personality traits from the colour of their auras is very controversial, because they vary so much from exponent to exponent.

The Rosenheim photograph is the only one in this book of alleged poltergeist activity, which is characterized by the moving of furniture and other phenomena caused by an unseen force. More than 40 witnesses swore to what they saw, video recorded the swinging lights you can see, and thorough investigations were done by authorities from the scientific and parapsychology establishment. This event might still be a mystery but no one can say it didn't happen. It's a pity we didn't think to include a DVD with this book...but there's a great idea for the next one.

The photographs that sum up the conundrums presented in this chapter the most are those taken by Dr. Baraduc. Immediately after his wife, and then his son, died he took photographs hoping to prove the body has a spirit that survives, but slowly departs. When you look at them every manner of thought possible will go through your mind. What sort of man was he to do such a thing so soon after bereavement? Is it a case of fraud, careless film development, or a technical camera fault? Was there an element of thoughtography, of aura transmission perhaps? Eventually, you will have to ask yourself if you believe in the continuation of the human soul.

A Spirit of Faith

LOCATION: The Holy Heart Hospital, location unknown
DATE: published September 15, 1992

'Father in Heaven – this is a human soul!' That was the reaction of a priest at The Holy Heart Hospital when shown this photograph. An article by Donald Rivers in *Weekly World News* in 1992 also said it showed 'a glowing angelic spirit rising up off the operating table' just as 32-year-old Karin Fischer died and her heart monitor went flat. Peter Valentin, the hospital's director of education, found the image among 72 photographs he took during the operation, and authenticated it. None of the 12 theatre staff saw anything at the time but surgeon Dr. Walter Springer and the biblical scholar Dr. Martin Muller have all been involved in subsequent discussion and research. Pope John Paul II requested a copy of the picture and 'clergymen and scholars throughout Europe' have investigated it. Well, that is the story.

> 'a glowing angelic spirit rising up off the operating table'

However, doubts about this well-known photograph arise quickly because the spirit image is so startlingly familiar. The crossed feet make it look suspiciously like a doctored crucifixion image has been added to the original operating theatre photograph by double exposure. Worryingly, despite the apparent provenance often quoted with this photograph, I can find no Holy Heart Hospital that exists and neither Dr. Springer nor Dr. Muller is detectable. But Donald Rivers was a fictional investigative journalist in *The Outer Limits*, a sci-fi television series created in the 1960s, and revived in the 1990s. This is just the sort of paranormal subject he would have relished. Ultimately, I believe each observer will accept the image or reject it based on their personal faith, unless they are a regular reader of *Weekly World News* which published the image. This specialist in spoofs also publishes regular stories of Elvis sightings, of George Bush planning to be the next Pope, and of an affair and marriage between Saddam Hussein and Osama bin Laden.

The Releasing of the Soul

LOCATION: Deathbed of Baraduc's wife, France
DATE: 1907

There was a 20-minute gap between these two plates of film capturing an intensely personal deathbed scene. Their similarity is what seems both most chilling and convincing: three clumps of mist hover over the recently dead body. Dr. Baraduc believed he had caught the soul of his wife departing. Hyppolite Baraduc had experimented with spirit photography in late 19th-century France, and also found early examples of what was later coined 'thoughtography'. Someone would concentrate on an image while holding an unexposed photographic plate and an image would appear on it, allegedly psychically. He addressed the French Academy of Medicine on the subject in 1895 and claimed to have invented a 'biometer', which could measure a nervous force and unknown forms of energy outside the human body. His findings about what he called the 'vital force' were published extensively and he wrote a book, *The Human Soul*, in Paris, in 1913.

If you believe that thoughtography is possible then it is likely that Baraduc's elevated emotional state of mind at his time of bereavement could have contributed to the creation of these images. On the other hand, it might have contributed to him making mistakes he did not recollect. But it's the similarity of the soul images that suggests another more mundane explanation. A professional photographer I contacted suggested miniscule pinholes in the bellows behind the lens of an early camera might produce such an effect, especially in an unstable environment on a long exposure. Their uniformity might be because such tiny holes were on one of the bellows' crease lines, the most delicate part of all and very prone to cracking.

'Dr. Baraduc believed he had caught the soul of his wife departing'

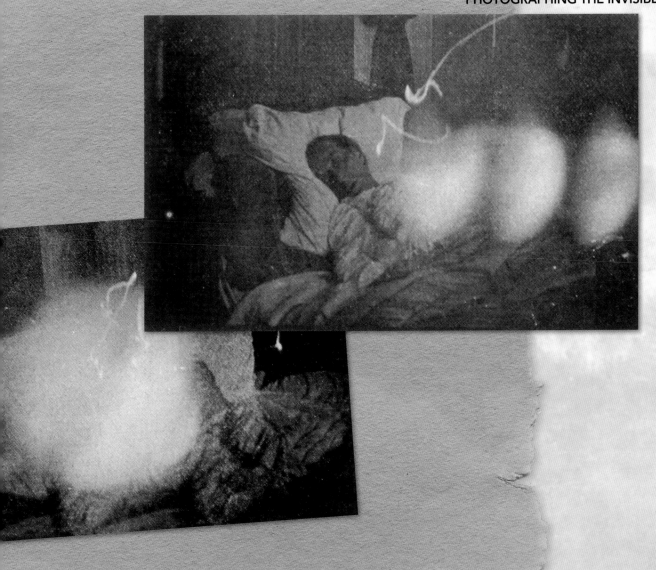

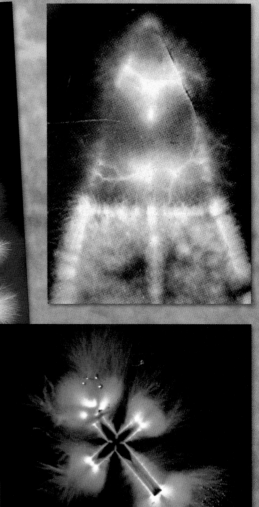

Mystery of the Reattached Leaf Tip

LOCATION: Russia
DATE: 1960s

Do such images prove that all living things produce an aura? These fascinating pictures were produced using a method discovered in Russia in 1939 by scientists Semyon and Valentina Kirlian. Their technique claims to capture the electrical energy currents of living things. To do so, the subject must be in direct contact with the film, 'sandwiched' between two metal plates and then a high-voltage charge is passed through it, which is said to amplify natural biological-energy flows. The effect of this amplification is then recorded directly on to film, giving the sort of results you see opposite. It was also claimed that the technique can recapture the human aura on film, but this is now disputed by the majority of investigators.

In 1966 the Russian researcher Victor Adamenko discovered that by cutting part of a leaf away, and then photographing the original using the Kirlian technique, an outline of the complete shape was still evident, albeit less clearly, as in the smaller green image, left. He continued his exploration and later found a Kirlian image of a human finger, for instance, would change colour according to the stress level of the person concerned. If true, this technique would obviously have medical implications and some practitioners have used it in this way, believing it can demonstrate the effectiveness of acupuncture.

'an outline of the complete shape was still evident'

The sceptical say the effects are possibly caused by moisture in or on the subjects photographed, or by the printing emulsions being displaced during printing. It would also be comparatively simple to produce such images using masking and double-exposure techniques. The image featuring a cross is another example of Kirlian photography, but this time the object is inanimate. The radiation or aura allegedly shows the psychological balance of the wearer of the cross and his or her relationship with it.

In the Highways of the Mind

LOCATION: Probably Denver, Colorado, USA
DATE: 1960s

This clear image of a double-decker bus was allegedly created solely by the projected concentration of Ted Serios' mind energy to make psychic photography or thoughtography. Serios was discovered in 1961, and from 1964 until 1967, Denver psychiatrist, Julie Eisenbud, experimented with him and a Model 95 Polaroid Land camera with black and white film. Serios held the closed camera between his legs, pointed it at his forehead and often used a 'gizmo', a tube of black paper directly on the camera to guide his thoughts more accurately. Many images seemed to be from postcards or books Serios had seen, rather than from pure imagination.

'he did produce plenty of images when many yards from the camera'

Sceptics believed the gizmo allowed Serios to use sleight-of-hand, but he did produce plenty of images when yards from the camera. In fact, this image was produced when Dr. John F. Conger, Dean of the University of Colorado Medical School, held his hand over the gizmo. Sometimes others tripped the camera, at other times Serios was put into a Faraday cage, a metallic enclosure that prevents the entry or escape of an electromagnetic (EM) field, or had to wear clothing provided to avoid objects being concealed. Serios was an alcoholic, he performed best when drunk, exhibited little self-control, and was said to 'wail and bang his head on the floor when things were not going his way'. His talent declined and finally disappeared after 1969. Serios created more than one thousand thoughtographs, and the implacably convinced (but widely debunked) Eisenbud challenged anyone to replicate the same effects, with or without trickery. The challenge was never accepted and noted psychic-sceptic James Randi said, 'If Mr. Serios ... did not use a trick method, all the rules of physics, particularly of optics, everything developed by science over the past several centuries, must be rewritten.'

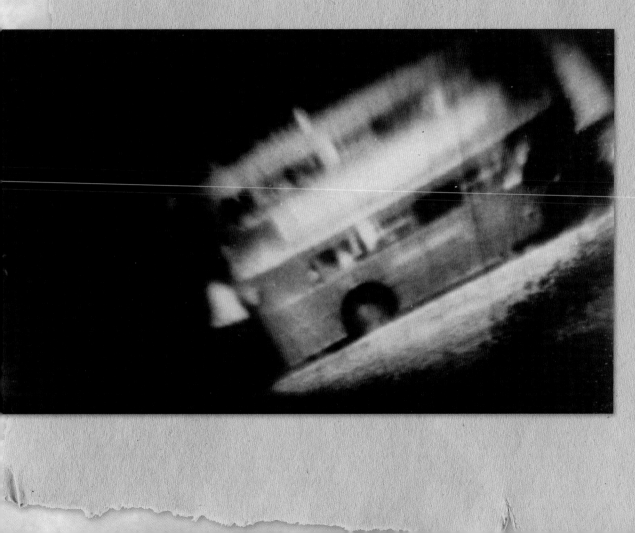

The Schneider Poltergeist

LOCATION: Königstrasse 13, Rosenheim, Bavaria, Germany
DATE: 1967/8

Whenever 18-year-old Anne-Marie Schneider was around, there were unexplainable noises and frightening phenomena, like these swinging lights captured on videotape. More than 40 people experienced them. In the lawyers' office where she worked, lights exploded unexpectedly and there were countless calls to the talking clock nobody claimed to have made. Then paintings and heavy furniture changed position by themselves. After technicians from Siemens and the Elektrizitätswerk (the German electricity board) couldn't find faults, physicists Dr. Karger of the Max Planck Institute of Plasma Physics and Dr. Zicha from Munich University could only say an unknown form of energy was at work. Then parapsychologist Hans Bender from the Freiburg Institute realized Anne-Marie Schneider seemed to trigger the phenomena and in 1968 made the video recordings.

Poltergeist action, a term covering unexplained noises and the physical moving of furniture, is generally associated with children and young people, especially if they are distressed. Anne-Marie was apparently unhappy at home and disliked her job. The movements ceased when she was eventually married in the 1970s. Nobody seems able to explain if poltergeist or psychokinetic incidents, where things are moved and sounds are made allegedly by the power of someone's mind, are conscious or unconscious. But this is an important picture documenting phenomenon notoriously difficult to photograph. Anne-Marie's baffling case is certainly worthy of further study.

'there were unexplainable noises and frightening phenomena, like these swinging lights'

New Ages of Enlightenment

LOCATION: (far left) Unknown; (near left) Stansted Hall, Stansted, Essex, England
DATE: 1990s

Do we all have an aura, an emanation of rays, which can be used to interpret our mental and physical health? Guy Coggins began photographing auras in the 1970s, using his biofeedback Aura Imager camera. The subject places their hands on metal sensors, which electronically interprets their aura. A polaroid system records their 'colours', but there is no claim actually to photograph the aura. Mediums and others interpret the subject's health, personality, or other matters from the variations of colour produced. When my aura was photographed my face was virtually obliterated by a red aura (near left) whereas others were shades of green, yellow, or blue. My aura was called 'the mask', and said to show I was somewhat sceptical, therefore psychically stopping my energy flow. The far left photograph shows the more customary effect: the woman's upper body is clearly visible, but above her head an explosion of auric energy can also be seen. The clarity of this shot suggests a healthy person of an extrovert nature.

In the digital-image age, most people have forgotten that colours from Polaroid prints change according to the speed of development and can thus be arranged to coincide with predestined outcomes, or be totally random if the developer is inept. There are also many problems with interpreting auras. In some New Age magazines the articles offer a baffling number of contrasting explanations for the same colours. The only consistent links between body, soul and colour are those of the Hindu chakras of the human body, with their seven identified energy centres.

'above her head an explosion of auric energy can also be seen'

175

The Orbs of Avebury Stone Circle

LOCATION: Avebury, Wiltshire, England
DATE: 1990s

Intriguingly, although often dismissed as an optic effect caused by a digital camera, these floating orbs have been seen by the naked eye. These alleged initial sightings make sceptical explanations ring very hollow indeed. It is true that reports of such floating orbs did increase in the 1990s, at the time digital cameras were being taken up. Other examples were digitally recorded at the nearby Red Lion pub, in 1994.

Sceptics opine the orbs are natural particles, like dust or water droplets, which have been dramatically enhanced by close flashlight and the digital process. Believers counter that the orbs seen with the naked eye have also been recorded on film and on video. The paranormal explanations of the origin of the orbs range from spirit manifestations to precisely the sort of unknown, supernatural energies you expect in such an enchanting place as the Avebury Stone Circle. Well worth a detour.

'precisely the sort of unknown, supernatural energies you expect'

Photographic Phenomena

LOCATION: Chelmsford, Essex, England
DATE: 1960s

Suddenly, happy faces of what must have been spirits were appearing on photographic plates, which were said to have been previously unopened. So were disjointed body parts, and even a building, later found to exist in St. Albans, in Hertfordshire, England. The astonished recipients of these alleged images from the other side were a group of spiritualists who met regularly in the 1960s. The phenomena of images appearing during séances on unused photographic plates and later on film was dubbed 'skotography' (Greek for dark-writing), by Miss Felicia Scatcherd, who died in 1927. Many of the Chelmsford skotographs were acquired by the late Cyril Permutt and donated to the Society for Psychical Research. In an unexplainable coincidence his son now owns a shop on the site of the building in St. Albans.

People are still claiming phenomena of this nature occur. Recent examples were produced in Scole, in Norfolk, England, where a group produced skotographs. In 1982 James Randi, noted psychic investigator, reported he tricked one skotograph artist at a séance into switching marked papers, and found the intended target had already been pre-exposed with a supposed spirit face. And couldn't the skotograph seen here simply be exposed and discarded stock, a photographic plate that had also been degraded by age and the incursion of light or damp? That might explain the inclusion of the St. Albans building in the Chelmsford images.

'The phenomena of images appearing during séances on unused photographic plates was dubbed "skotography"'

What Happened to Tinkerbell?

LOCATION: Penrith, Cumbria, England
DATE: 1994

Do some animals possess senses we human beings have lost, or never had in the first place? This photograph of Tinkerbell apparently in the grip of a curious energy force, while Bunty seems not to care, raises many questions. When the negative and the print were sent to the Society for Psychical Research the question was: 'Do you think it's a trick of the camera or was something paranormal happening?' So far no one has been able to answer. One photographic expert I asked had seen the red-line effect before, but 'never with a distortion as appears with the cat's face…There may be a natural explanation but I don't know of one.'

> 'there may be a natural explanation but I don't know of one'

The reason for taking the shot is not known and it would be useful to discover what else was going on. For instance, was the child on the sofa taunting or playing with the cats? If the paranormal solution is not accepted, the alternative is rather implausible; an extraordinary coincidence of a lighting or developing problem on the film, exactly where Tinkerbell was tilting her head. Such coincidences must occur, of course, but that doesn't mean we should leave it at that and not also accept the likelihood of an unexplainable paranormal moment having been captured on film. I think it no coincidence cats have been associated with good and bad luck for as long as they have been domesticated. The Egyptians believed them to be sacred, even godlike. We are still not sure how these ancients built the Pyramids, so perhaps there are other mysteries they knew about cats…and about parallel worlds.

A simulacrum is anything that has a superficial likeness to something else. This chapter contains examples that are probably not paranormal but dramatically stretch the bounds of credibility, demanding you make up your mind about what you are observing. Seeing significant shapes while staring into flames or cloud formations are pastimes we have probably all enjoyed at some stage of our lives. As children we think the Man in the Moon might be real and, if we have been moved by stories of witches in folklore and fairytales, sometimes fear what we think we see in the shapes of trees on dark winter nights. That inner need to make sense of something we don't immediately understand, or which can be interpreted in both good and bad ways, is the basis of the Rorschach inkblot test used by psychology and psychiatry researchers. What subjects say they see in the blots is used to interpret personality traits, using the practicality or bizarreness of their interpretations to help identify their mental state. The outstanding question is whether or not shapes and what they seem to represent can have a paranormal element to them and if they do, are the messages we take helpful and beneficial to the running of our lives?

The alleged sightings of religious figures, most notably of Jesus and the Virgin Mary, have been reported throughout history and it is not therefore surprising to find them appearing in photographs. There were many images of Jesus I could have chosen for the book, and only slightly fewer of the Virgin Mary. An interesting fact I have noticed is that simulacra of the Virgin Mary seem to glow, apparently with a holy light.

An especially charming picture is the one construed as showing the face of a cherub, a baby angel, in the posy of flowers held by a bridesmaid. Paintings we

have seen in churches, galleries, and in books have unquestionably conditioned us to have a certain expectation of what a cherub should look like. It could be that presented with a shape it doesn't understand, our brain gives us the most comforting explanation it can, and that in reality they probably do not exist. Even if they do, we don't see them often enough to be able to say, 'This is what a cherub really looks like'. However, to my mind, it's a rather enchanting picture and it always brings a smile when I show it to people. What is astonishing is how detailed the modelling of the face appears to be. And yet it is clearly the folds and shadows of the flowers. A coincidence surely, but what a coincidence. The image certainly has the power to move people, whatever the truth might be. That can't be denied or ignored.

The Belméz faces are an interesting case which perhaps moves beyond the coincidence of a momentary 'trick of the light'. They began to appear in the concrete floor of a small house in Andalucia, in Spain, during 1971. They were photographed extensively and submitted to numerous tests. In the end there was no agreement about how they could have been made fraudulently, and so perhaps they were genuinely paranormal events. Here, your personal belief system takes over. If you admit no possibility of the paranormal then an explanation of fraud or mere coincidence will satisfy you. If you believe unknown forces using energies we still do not understand are possible, then you are justified in accepting them as paranormal.

When you are exploring the paranormal, the simplest or most comforting answer is not always the right answer.

The Madonna of the Fountain

LOCATION: Center Parcs Holiday Village, Norfolk, England
DATE: c.1995

This startling photograph caused a sensation at the time, and no wonder. The outline seen in the fountain could hardly be anything other than a Madonna and Child. The outline of the cloak seems unmistakable and so does its unworldly radiance. And look at the swaddled baby in her arms. He seems to be transparent, supernatural, just as you'd expect of the Christ-child.

'the cloak seems unmistakable and so does its unworldly radiance'

Moving water is often associated with the apparent appearance of spirits, especially those associated with religion. Its imagery of purification, its sparkling clarity, and swirling movements are positive and life-affirming factors making something we think we see much more acceptable than, say, a possible ghost in a cemetery. So yes, this might be one of the rare pictures taken of a Marian appearance. But there are times when our brain translates something it does not understand into something familiar, even if it is actually fooling both itself and you. It's a way of reducing fear, tension, and unfounded suspicion. A way of bringing order to chaos.

A Cherub Posing in a Wedding Posy?

LOCATION: Unknown
DATE: 1960s

It's a picture I always show without prior comment when giving talks on anomalous or unusual photographs. Not everyone spots it straight away, but hundreds of people have immediately seen the face gazing out from the top of the girl's wedding posy as a charming cherub. Cyril Permutt, an important 20th-century psychic researcher, was sent this photograph in 1980 by the girl's aunt who felt some concern about it. Mr. Permutt replied encouragingly, saying he believed the image was not harmful in any way, adding, 'this photograph shows signs of psychic or paranormal influence.' Certainly no one I have shown it to has felt it harbours anything unpleasantly psychic or 'harmful'. It seems more often to be regarded as something holy, no doubt because this is generally the quality attributed to cherubs and other angels. This makes the bridesmaid a refreshing antidote to some of the more diabolical images in this book. If you'd like to see more alleged images of angels I recommend the website *angelsghosts.com*.

I can't say for certain that a tiny angelic creature has hidden in the flowers on this happy day and then artlessly popped out for a look just as the shot was taken. I've included it because it's a very good example of a simulacrum or superficial likeness that is hard to explain in normal ways. And because it makes so many people feel good.

'this photograph shows signs of psychic or paranormal influence'

The Virgin in the Trees

LOCATION: Near Metz, Alsace, France
DATE: Unknown

There is definitely a startling draped figure here that looks like the Virgin Mary, high in the tree on the left of the church. This image has never been claimed to be the physical presence of the Mother of Christ but something visionary, inspirational rather than devotional. The image is a particular rarity because although thought to appear often, Marian visions are rarely photographed (I have included one other on page 89, captured in Karácsond, Hungary). Other appearances, without photographs, have famously included Medjugorje, in Croatia, and Lourdes, in France, both of which have a vast literature documenting the appearances. Less well known is the appearance of her image in a tree in Watsonville, California, reported in the *Fortean Times* in 1997.

The Roman Catholic faith is usually very sceptical about these sightings and Popes have been hesitant to grant paranormal or saintly status unless the evidence is absolutely conclusive. The stereotypical iconography of the modestly veiled Virgin Mary with Jesus in her arms is commonly spotted in caves and other rock formations, even in water, as seen on page 53. These can be simply explained by her image being more easily recognizable than, say, Joseph. Yet, looking again, the image could be of him or any other biblical character. When you look closely to see how the wall of the church and the trunk of the tree define the shape, you are compelled to interpret the picture as a coincidence of viewpoint. But is it not remarkable how perfectly it holds together, with the branches tracing the drapery of the Virgin's robes?

'Marian visions are rarely photographed'

Indelible Faces in the Floor

LOCATION: Bélmez de la Moraleda, Andalucia, Spain
DATE: August 23, 1971

These pictures are certainly inexplicable and I defy anyone not to be mystified or moved. In fact they have been dubbed 'the most important paranormal phenomenon' of the 20th century. In 1971 a remarkable discovery was made by Doña Maria Gómez Pereira. On the concrete floor of the kitchen in her small house in the Andalucian village of Bélmez there was a face gazing up at her. It appeared to be painted, yet was resistant to scratching. Her son Miguel broke up the flooring because they found it disturbing and then new concrete was laid. Within a week the same image had returned. This attracted so much publicity the mayor ordered it to be cut out and kept behind glass and soon hundreds were visiting the house to see it and others, which slowly appeared. Meanwhile excavation discovered human bones and the haunting realization that most of the street was built over a graveyard. During the following months other faces appeared and a total figure of 18 was declared at one point. None of the faces were susceptible to any cleaning agent and couldn't be scratched. When some were covered with a transparent film for protection they continued to change, seen as proof of paranormal origins.

'excavation discovered human bones and the haunting realization that most of the street was built over a graveyard'

The Bélmez Faces have been very extensively researched and tested. Although signs of brush marks were detected, opinions differed on the presence of paint. The general view is the images were created by using chemicals which bonded atomically with the structure of the concrete and were light sensitive, like the silver nitrate used in traditional photography, thus explaining the slow appearance and fading. Yet even though there seems to be scientific consensus about fakery, no one has come up with a convincing, universally acceptable explanation for the faces of Bélmez. Perhaps there isn't one?

Christ in the Alpine Snow

LOCATION: Swiss Alps
DATE: 1958

The photographer of this picture was an atheist until he had a sudden strange compulsion to take a shot through the window of the plane in which he was travelling. What he captured made him a believer immediately. This stylized portrait of Christ, seemingly formed by snow and rocks, is certainly a startling simulacrum, and its mystic quality cannot be immediately dismissed or quickly forgotten. Neither has it been. It was first published in 1958, was repeated in 1965, and then used as 'the most famous picture we have ever printed' in the *Sunday People*'s five-thousandth issue in 1977.

> '**What he captured made him a believer immediately**'

The popular press enjoys publishing such controversial pictures, making no profound claim for them and taking no responsibility for their veracity. They attract attention and so sell papers and magazines, and the media says it is ultimately the public's choice whether they believe the images are what they appear to be. As with most of the images in this chapter, the circumstances of the picture do not particularly encourage the belief that there is some sort of supernatural presence or apparition. It is surely a coincidence – a trick of the light. Nevertheless, one can hardly help marvelling at such a coincidence.

Sacred Elephant in the Sky

LOCATION: Chiang Mai, Northern Thailand
DATE: 1994

David Shurville didn't recognize the white, elephant-shaped cloud until his film had been developed. But there it is, exactly where anyone interested in Buddhism and the paranormal would want it to be, ideally positioned over the golden chedi, or spire, of an important temple's pagoda, which is supported by more massive carved elephants. It could hardly be thought more sacred or more propitious. This is because before Buddha was born his mother is alleged to have dreamed of a white elephant and so they are closely associated with great events and good luck. Thus the very rare birth of a white elephant is treated as especially auspicious, and in Thailand such animals always become the property of the monarch.

Of course, looking for shapes in clouds is something we have all enjoyed, and so have people throughout history. For instance, a painting by Piero Della Francesca of 1460 from his *Légende de la Croix* series shows a cloud formation that has been interpreted as showing flying saucers. The *Fortean Times* regularly prints pictures of clouds readers have interpreted to their advantage or disadvantage. What you think depends on what you believe about there being another world, which can sometimes break through the separating veils to warn or encourage us. It's very comforting to think so, and there's just as much evidence for as there is against.

'It could hardly be thought more sacred or more propitious'

The Tumbling Ghost of Lavardin

LOCATION: Church in Lavardin, near Vendôme, France
DATE: September, 1990

The moving but shapeless phantasm is curious and convincing enough, but turn the page upside down and it's much more clearly human, angelic even, perhaps caught in the middle of a joyous paranormal tumble. The photographer, a Mr. Culley, confirmed the apparition was only on one of a number of pictures he took at the same time. The shot was sent to Dr. Vernon Harrison, an ex-president of the Royal Photographic Society and expert on anomalous photographs. He wrote:

'The "clouds" here are wholly confined to the picture frame and are not due to leakage of light into the film cassette. In all the other pictures the behaviour of film and camera is quite normal. The structure of the "cloud" does not suggest it results from internal reflections of bright light within the lens or camera body … Uneven development would not affect just one frame leaving all the others perfect.'

'it is hard to find a rational explanation for the anomaly'

In fact, it's agreed all round that it is hard to find a rational explanation for the anomaly. It is tempting to think that it might be somehow caused by light streaming in from the upper window, and in 2007 it was suggested to me it could simply be a tissue or something similar wafting though the air that was caught on this picture and is thus another case of photographer blindness. Actually, calling the image the Tumbling or Upside-Down Ghost can be very unhelpful when searching for a truth about something puzzling. Expectations have already been aroused by the nature of the subject and the easy pleasure of finding what one is looking for is something encouraged by both our conscious and unconscious minds. But if a clever name stops us looking harder or thinking further the real mystery might be obfuscated, lost to us forever.

The Mystery of Brixton's Shroud Image

LOCATION: Mostyn Road Methodist Church, Brixton, London, England
DATE: First noticed in 1948

Whatever your faith or belief system there's little doubt that the image of the man's face on the wall is startlingly similar to that on the famous Turin Shroud, the cloth supposedly wound around Christ's body after he was taken from the Cross. The photograph was sent to the Society for Psychical Research only in 1995 with a very brief covering note that frustratingly left many questions unanswered. However, the letter approached the subject with a very common-sense attitude, neither implying nor inferring anything. We can probably conclude from this at least that the photographer does not seem to have been motivated by his own beliefs and was simply recording what he saw.

In 1948 when this shot was most likely taken, the magnificently spired Mostyn Road Methodist Church was awaiting restoration after it had been very badly damaged during the Second World War. The area of wall or ceiling appears to have survived undamaged and is above a curtained area which may have been an altar. It's not known what the markings are; they could be bomb damage or simply damp or mould.

> **'startlingly similar to that on the famous Turin Shroud'**

Often a suggested interpretation tells us more about the character of the photographer or the reporter than the actual image itself. One person sees the face of Christ or God, perhaps also believing in some direct personal contact, whilst another sees a damp patch on the wall. If a believer in the Christian faith wishes to accept this was indeed a sign of some holy presence, then who am I to contradict it in the absence of other evidence?

Disembodied Faces in the Waves

LOCATION: from SS *Watertown*, Pacific Ocean
DATE: December 1924

James Courtney and Michael Meehan were buried at sea on December 4, 1924 while they were working on board the U.S. tanker SS *Watertown*, after gas fumes suffocated them. It is said images of the men first appeared on the side of the ship from which they had been committed. Then it is alleged several crew members saw their disembodied ghostly heads in the waves, about forty feet away and for up to ten seconds at a time. On a return journey through the same waters, the ship's captain, Keith Tracey, took a set of six photographs. When shipping company employee James Patton had the film developed in New York, one of the shots showed the faces of the two men in the sea. The camera and film were investigated by the Burns Detective Agency and found to be genuine, and psychical researcher, Hereward Carrington, could only suggest the faces might have been 'thought-forms' or thought photographs, created by strong images of the dead men in the onlookers' minds.

Unfortunately the original photograph cannot be found, making much scrutiny of the image purely speculative. One of my problems is how similar the two faces appear, both wearing moustaches and both with very sunken, black eyes, but perhaps that's how many men looked at the time. The out-of-focus problem means waves or rocks may have produced this illusion, but this can't be checked because no one knows now if these images appeared close to a coast or well out at sea. Anyway, each of the reports of the sightings is quite different, making the photograph an eternal mystery.

'ghostly heads in the waves, about forty feet away'

EVERYDAY ANOMALIES

Most of the pictures in this chapter, and most of the best examples of 'ghost' photographs, were not taken by investigators staking out haunted locations in the hope of capturing something strange on camera. They were taken by ordinary people and intended to be of ordinary things – simple snaps of friends and family. But then, and often after having forgotten about them for some time, they noticed something strange, something anomalous on the image that should not, surely could not, be there. In many cases they sent their pictures to organizations like the Society for Psychical Research and the photographs and the stories that came with them were subjected to close scrutiny. Often this provided a simple explanation. But not always.

Many of our selection here have not appeared in print before. None of them seems to have an obviously fraudulent origin and I have sought as much detail as possible about the places and circumstances. On the technical side I sought the help of professional photographers who alerted me to many possible explanations of strange appearances in photographs. These include camera shake or subject movement creating blurring; lighting flare and light trails forming fogs or shafts of light; hair on or near the lens; dust or pollen in the air; imperfections in film or during the development process; and even the effect of smoke or breath. I learned to be especially wary of 'camera-strap syndrome', where a part of the strap falls unnoticed over the lens and, because it is so close, leaves a blurry and indistinct smudge on the photograph. That's amazingly common. Once you add deliberate fraud to that list, mistaken identity and defective memory, it seems a wonder any photograph ever manages to remain unexplained or anomalous. But some do.

Supposing you are presented with something anomalous, potentially paranormal, I would urge you to try to photograph it if possible.

EVERYDAY ANOMALIES

Simple advice to avoid the above mentioned pitfalls would be to make sure that you hold the camera very still – hold your breath when you press the shutter – avoid using flash and check that no stray hair, cigarette smoke, or the camera strap is compromising the shot. Maurice Townsend also advises that if you are using a Polaroid or digital camera, which shows results at once, then take several frames. This will either confirm the presence of the anomaly, something for which any investigator will be exceptionally grateful, or show it to be a one-shot mystery.

For serious photographers on location and with the time to prepare, it's a good idea to have a 'witness' camera. Simon Earwicker suggests using two cameras synchronized together with a cable release. One should have a flash and one without, and ideally one should have a wide-angle lens. This way the simultaneous images will immediately reveal whether a technical problem is the cause of the anomaly. And if two pictures show the anomaly from a different angle it eliminates the possibility that it is a trick of the light dependent on viewpoint.

As you read this chapter I would particularly encourage you to use the investigative guidelines given in the introduction. And then you might want to explore your own photograph albums and boxes, your discs and videos to see if you possess any anomalous shots of your own.

205

Black Abbot in a Haunted Graveyard

LOCATION: St. Mary's churchyard, Prestbury, Gloucestershire, England
DATE: November 22, 1990

The village of Prestbury, near Cheltenham, in Gloucestershire, is a popular location for alleged sightings of ghosts and other paranormal activity. As early as 1981 it was being referred to as 'The Most Haunted Village' in competition with the other famously haunted village of Pluckley, in Kent, and a current BBC website draws attention to its various paranormal phenomena. This spooky image was captured when, Derek Stafford, a photographer, was taking shots of the floodlit gravestones in St. Mary's churchyard. He was sure that no-one else was present in the graveyard as he did this, but on subsequent development the film image of a black hooded figure (the ghostly abbot?) appeared on the last slide.

According to Richard Jones (in *Haunted Britain and Ireland*, 2001) the Black Abbot, 'appears most often at Christmas, Easter and All Souls Day.' The ghost evidently passes through the graveyard before disappearing through the wall of Reform Cottage in the High Street, whereupon poltergeist activity is heard emanating from the attic. Further stories tell of knocks being heard on the door and of a passage that links the 16th-century cottage with the nearby church – possibly used as an escape route for the monks in difficult times. The garden may have been used as a burial ground when the church owned the surrounding property. It is not known why the abbot would be haunting this area unless he still feels that he is attached to the property in some timeless link.

> **'the ghost passes through the graveyard before disappearing through the wall of Reform Cottage'**

A Ghostly Arm-pull in Manila

LOCATION: Manila, Philippines
DATE: 2000s

Is this ghostly figure trying to get in the picture? Does the spirit have some connection with the girls? The correct scale of the figure and the exact placement of their hand on the girls arm seems to make an accidental double exposure unlikely. These Filipino good friends were strolling in a newly developed part of Manila and decided they wanted a shot to record their time together. One of them asked a total stranger to take a picture, using the camera of a Nokia 7250 phone. The astonishing result shows a phantasmic figure pulling at the arm of the girl on the right. The shot was aquired via The Ghost Research Society and they report that neither of the girls was aware of anything strange happening at the time, and that it 'seems to be quite a friendly spirit'. The hold on the arm appears to be quite firm, not a gentle touch, so if it were somehow a real person you would expect her to be reacting. Some say the phantom arm-puller looks like a woman, others that it's a man, but the lack of malevolence is generally agreed upon.

It's hard to be certain in this digital age, but it's considered unlikely you could make a double-exposure on the camera of a phone. Yet with a digital image, it would be the easiest thing in the world for a computer whiz to have doctored the original shot. The answer of course would be to interview the girls. But who are they? Do you know them? Are you one of them? We are waiting for your call.

> **'a phantasmic figure pulling at the arm of the girl on the right'**

Birthday Intruders

LOCATION: Bromsgrove, Worcestershire, England
DATE: February 23, 1993

Look who has also come to the party uninvited. Phillip Fowler has taken a flash photograph of son Matthew waiting to blow out his birthday candles, and disembodied faces seem to be floating out of the cake, but are corpselike and certainly not interested in what's about to happen. Mr. Fowler sent this photograph to the Society for Psychical Research seeking no publicity for the shot, but simply asking for clarification of the birthday-party intruders. He used a Hanimex focus-free 35mm self-winding camera with flash and with the lights off to enhance the candles on the cake. He took a picture directly before this one with the lights on, but it included no unusual extra figures. The negatives were examined and the company processing the images could not explain how the faces appeared and claimed no tampering had taken place. Another photographic expert thought the extra image to be a reflection from a television set. None of the Fowlers' friends or family could identify the mysterious 'intruders' and Matthew says he did not experience anything strange at the time.

'disembodied faces seem to be floating out of the cake, corpselike'

In my experience, people are often unsettled by this image. If the circumstances in which it was produced are true, this photograph certainly appears to show something very strange indeed, truly anomalous. Every one of the neutral observers I've shown it to, people who neither believe in the paranormal nor hold anything against the possibility of unknown phenomena existing, has been intrigued and, sometimes, disturbed. It would help if someone could identify the biggest head. Can you?

A Baffling Presence on Calvary Hill

LOCATION: Church of the Holy Sepulchre, Jerusalem, Israel
DATE: c. 1990

Visiting the Church of the Holy Sepulchre is always a spiritual experience. It's built over the site of Calvary Hill, where Christians believe Jesus Christ was crucified. But would you expect to capture what looks like a real spirit on film? The in-laws of Mrs. Thompson of Dunstable, Bedfordshire, England, thought nothing of their snap, but Mrs. Thompson thought it showed a ghostly nun. Maurice Grosse, the Chairman of the Spontaneous Cases Committee for the Society for Psychical Research, replied to her saying:

'The cloud effect could be construed as the result of a double exposure due to a fault with the camera … However, the configuration … does not seem to justify this conclusion … The base of the 'cloud' clearly shows two shoes, complete with laces, and what could be construed as a hand or foot stretching forward … there appears to be a shadow on the lower part of the left hand [sic] shoe … This cloud type effect is not unknown … in places of religious significance, but it is most unusual to see such detail … it is certainly one of the strangest configurations I have seen …'

> 'certainly one of the strangest configurations I have seen'

I first thought a cat had walked through the shot. But closer scrutiny showed other light effects above the main image and the foot and shoe mentioned. There is also the chance of this being some curious play of light in dust in the air. But are those modern shoes, and why is it common for pictures like this to be 'not unknown … in places of religious significance?' Calvary Hill has more than one anomaly to give up.

Who is the Lady in Blue?

LOCATION: Woodcroft, Boar's Hill, Oxford, England
DATE: May 20, 1990

Does the second of these two photographs, taken moments apart, also include the young man's dead grandmother? His mother, Mrs. Seligman, believes the apparition is her late mother-in-law, wearing the low-heeled, dark shoes and blue or blue-grey skirt and woollen top she wore when she was alive. Photography expert Dr. Vernon Harrison, an ex-President of the Royal Photographic Society, had this to say:

'I can think of no normal explanation … The 'skirt-like' object is in a dark blue colour not found elsewhere in the picture and it is opaque … Below the 'skirt' emerges what appears to be a bare human right foot, the toes of which are clearly visible … could be interpreted as the figure of a child or diminutive woman, bare-footed and wearing a dark blue skirt extending almost to the ankles and a bluish-grey shawl … I do not think that any of the usual explanations (e.g. double exposure, stray light, misinterpretation of patterns, etc.) can apply here.'

I find it hard to dismiss such an opinion from Dr. Harrison. But if there are no technical problems with the photographs, and their backgrounds are identical except for the figure in the blue shawl, what other explanation is there? You know the answer.

'I do not think that any of the usual explanations can apply here'

The Little Girls

LOCATION: Near Beck Hole, North Yorkshire Moors, England
DATE: 11 August 1982

This was intended to be a picture of a little girl playing by a stream, but turned out to be something much more mysterious. After development, and clearly shown on the negative, was what appeared to be another girl or girls in Victorian or Edwardian dress in the background. The father of the small girl shown in the foreground took this photograph between 2pm and 3pm on a hot sunny afternoon when no one else was in view. It is not known who or what it is, but the photographer is certain the anomaly was not there when he took the shot. Professional photographer and psychic investigator Cyril Permutt was sufficiently intrigued to show this photograph to a medium who provided a reading from it. Apparently the medium could 'see' various figures in addition to the white form and was able to give specific dates. It was not reported whether the family of the girl found these to be significant.

'It is not known who or what it is, but the photographer is certain the anomaly was not there when he took the shot'

The idea that the anomalous figures are in historic dress appeals to the notion that the sighting of a ghost may be some sort of 'time slip': the ghost getting on with its own business in its own time but somehow momentarily visible to another time, a century later. This provides an interesting and logical explanation for the sightings of monks and nuns walking through ancient cloisters and other such traditional ghost stories.

Teacher Spectre in the Playground

LOCATION: Playground, somewhere in England
DATE: June 1977

These excited schoolchildren thought they were simply posing for a souvenir of their Silver Jubilee outing. What they didn't expect is people would be still looking at their photograph 30 years later. That's because a fleeting figure can clearly be seen behind the group moving from right to left, dressed in what appears to be a grey, full-skirted dress with a big white collar, and with her brown hair tied back in a bun. The baffling photograph was one of several taken at the time on an Ilford Sportsman camera. Mrs. Gregory, the photographer, was convinced there was no one behind the group and the shot taken immediately before (not shown here) seems to prove that. So what can the explanation be?

> **'a fleeting figure can clearly be seen behind the group'**

A photographic expert felt it was unlikely to be camera shake or a sticky shutter, because much more of the picture would be blurred. It's obviously a dull day and the shutter speed must have been quite slow but the children are all more or less in focus. This is a case where photographer's blindness must be suspected, that is, another person did indeed walk hurriedly behind the children but was not noticed through the lens. Yet look again. Doesn't the figure seem to be in rather old-fashioned clothes, the sort you'd expect a teacher from former times to wear? The possibilities of fraud or accident are both ways to resolve the problem, and so is a paranormal solution. Perhaps this really is a privileged glimpse of a departed but still unsettled teacher, doomed forever to anxiously patrol the children in her playground?

The Miraculous Madonna of Karácsond

LOCATION: Karácsond Church, near Budapest, Hungary
DATE: September 1989

This puzzling photograph is on display in the church where it was taken, a clear indication that priest Béla Kovács, and his congregation, believe a genuine miracle occurred here. They accept unquestioningly, as do many others, that it shows the Virgin Mary. Some see her holding the infant Jesus. Others think he stands in front of her. Contradictory claims say the image was captured either by a taxi driver or by the art restorer Károly Ligeti, who also says he actually saw this vision, not noticed by other people in the church, while standing on some scaffolding. The incumbent priest asserted there was no similar statue in the church that might have been catching the sun and thus creating a reflection that could be interpreted as such a vision.

Various organizations have studied the photograph, including the Hungarian Press Agency and Britain's Independent UFO Network and claim there had been no tampering. Unsurprisingly there are differing opinions, as you can see for yourself in issues of the *Fortean Times* in 1994 and 1996. These range from accusations of outright deception by Ligeti to a lighting or development gremlin. Those convinced of paranormal origins say genuine religious feelings allowed him to project a form of mind energy so powerful it could also be photographed. Janet Bord, the researcher of Fortean phenomena, wrote in the *Fortean Times* that an outright pronouncement of faking would be 'somewhat ill-judged and hasty'.
.

'a form of mind energy so powerful it could also be photographed'

Hooded Figure of Les Caves Huguenots

LOCATION: Huguenot Caves, Ardèche Region, France
DATE: October 1986

The glaring ethereal light could be just about anything, but the hand that emerges from it makes you wonder. The caves of the southwestern regions were once the main hiding places in France for Huguenots, Protestant worshippers who were banned by Louis IX. Their history of persecution is bloody and tragic. To anybody in the least sensitive, these caves positively reek of their turbulent history. Mrs. Keighly wanted only to photograph the ceiling stalactites and had asked to be left alone for a few moments in the lower cave to achieve a clear view. She felt and saw no one beside her. She took her pictures with a 'cheap Kodak disc camera' and these were developed by a photographer in Milford-on-Sea, Lymington, England. When she noticed the anomaly shown here, she sent the photograph to the Society for Psychical Research. Dr. Harrison researched the photograph and found it to be 'very curious'. He felt the 'hooded figure' could be 'the back view of a robed figure, wearing head dress Arab fashion', but that it could also be 'the effect of stray light'. However, several fingers appear to be emerging from the robes and resting on the safety rail, which he found baffling if this were simply a lighting manifestation. Dr. Harrison's conclusion was that the photograph should be consigned to the 'unexplained' file, as a definite anomaly.

Another photographic expert believes there must have been an object in the foreground Mrs. Keighly had inadvertently photographed, perhaps something also held in her hands and which had slipped into frame while she was concentrating on the roof formations, and then bleached out by the closeness of the flashlight. That's an easy explanation, but considering the history of the caves, could you be sure it was the right one? And why should it be Arabic headdress? Might not this just as plausibly be the

> 'To anybody in the least sensitive, these caves positively reek of their turbulent history'

The Puzzle of the Painted Monk

LOCATION: Haworth Moor, Yorkshire, England
DATE: February 2004

Is this a real place almost too picturesque to be true, and with a real ghost? Or is it a manipulated image that only owns up to its fraudulence when blown up? A Mrs. Friar sent the digital photograph to the Society for Psychical Research, saying:

> '… she [Mrs. Friar's niece] took several shots of Haworth Moor landscape for her current Art project and was curious, on downloading the following images, to see another figure which had certainly not been there when taking the picture … to me it is the "archetypal grey-hooded figure roaming the moors" (the figure appears quite ethereal compared to the man in black behind it on the path) …'

'the figure appears quite ethereal compared to the man in black'

Mrs. Friar and her art-student niece found the picture to be 'rather fanciful, but quite intriguing nevertheless'. Indeed. There are definitely some unexplained or unexplainable details open to many interpretations. There is a jagged black diagonal line behind the hooded figure and the 'real' man in black has a forked-lightning effect apparently ending in his hands, plus a curious brown shape behind him. These look like marks or tears consistent with an old print rather than a digital image. The most obvious possibility is the art student deviously manipulated the digital image as part of her course work, but didn't tell her aunt. Look at the close-up of the supposed monk and it looks very much as though he has been quickly, impressionistically painted in, as do the bracken and grasses. Of course the student simply might not have noticed someone else all wrapped up for a chilly February walk. Or, just possibly, she might have photographed the ghost of a lonely monk walking on the moors.

225

The Sleeping Ghost

LOCATION: Rossal House, Sunbury-on-Thames, Surrey, England
DATE: Unknown

There seems to be one blindingly obvious question here. Why would anyone looking for ghosts under test conditions take a photograph of a chair? Actually, there is a second one. Why would a ghost wrap itself in a blanket? This image is supposed to have been caught by inventor and electro-metallurgist Sherard Cowper-Coles during experiments with Admiral Moore, a member of the Ghost Club. It was taken in daylight in the sitting room where a vacant armchair, covered in pink and white striped chintz, stood by the window. There was no one else in the sitting room and the transparent figure has never been identified. It should be added that Cowper-Coles' wife, also a scientist, attested she had actually seen the ghost thought to haunt Rossal.

'she had actually seen the ghost thought to haunt Rossal'

The face itself is fascinating. The painted eyebrows and curly blonde hair look very much like the challenging fashions adopted by the young women of the 1920s and 30s, and Cowper-Coles died in 1936. Or do you think it more like a Georgian gentleman, bewigged and powdered? The photographers certainly thought it a man. Either way, the photograph has all the hallmarks of a simple double exposure, but would such worthy gentlemen be indulging in fraud, or unaware if a photographic mishap had occurred under their so-called test conditions? Anyway, wouldn't the gents or their friends have recognized the face if a living person were indeed involved? You have to ask, just who is the wrapped-up person resting their head so wearily on Cowper-Coles' chair? When did he or she live?

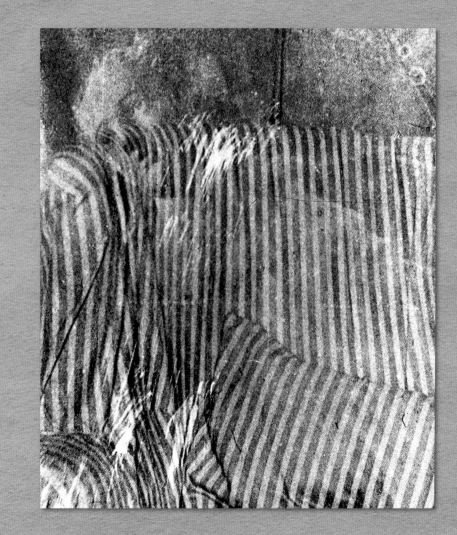

The Ghost of Hanging Tree

LOCATION: Cromdale Church, Morayshire, Scotland
DATE: October 9, 1976

Do you know what a real ghost looks like? It's not often they're like the vaporous, indistinct shapes depicted by Hollywood. In fact, most of the cases investigated by the Society for Psychical Research during the past 125 years have looked like you and me, just as they were when they were supposedly alive. So what's that in this photograph of an old tree at Cromdale Church, known as the 'hanging tree', captured by a Mrs. Ramsay? The reputation of the tree, formerly used as a gallows, is linked to the tale of a battle that took place here between the Grants and the Jacobites, and one of the tombstones does mark the grave of a member of the Grant family.

'Being hanged publicly would make a good case for this wraith being created by the terror of the victim'

There is a widely held belief that if there was extreme emotion at the time of someone's death, this will continue to stimulate inexplicable events for many years into the future. Being hanged publicly from a tree would make a good case for this wraith in Mrs. Ramsay's shot having been created by the terror of the victim. The great problem here is the lack of focus. It means this is just as likely to be a simulacrum, something unknown, but so like something we know that the brain explains it in terms we readily accept – rightly or wrongly. So, the blurry spectre could just be a trick of the light, but it certainly looks like a hanged corpse with a hooded head, as long as you believe this is what a ghost looks like.

The Watcher of St. Botolph's Balcony

LOCATION: St. Botolph's Church, Bishopsgate, London, England
DATE: May 15, 1982

Mr. and Mrs. Brackley had got themselves to the church well on time. He had come to photograph a wedding but, because they were early, secured permission to photograph the church's interior. He used a ten-second exposure on a tripod-mounted camera because of the lack of sufficient lighting. They were both adamant there was no one else in the church at the time and that there is no evidence that their equipment nor the development of the film was faulty. But they had been watched by a strange robed figure on the balcony in the top right of the picture.

> 'they had been watched by a strange robed figure'

St. Botolph's Church has a tragic history, as have many churches in London, with many unnamed plague victims of 1665 hurriedly buried unmarked in its graveyard. Because the spectral figure appears to be robed, and a wedding was about to take place, it's possible a member of the church's hierarchy or one of the choir did walk in briefly, notice the photographer and turn around, hoping not to have been spotted. How would someone up there know where the camera was pointed? If the picture is consciously fraudulent then a professional photographer like Brackley has the best chance of getting away with it. But listen to what is supposed to have happened some years later. A builder contacted Mr. Brackley, saying while he was working in St. Botolph's crypt he had accidentally disturbed some coffins, one of which was opened to reveal a body with a similar face to the one in his picture. This sensational message seems impossible, for surely a face in a coffin would be considerably deteriorated?

Unknown Hand in the Veil

LOCATION: St. Austin's Roman Catholic Church, Merseyside, Liverpool, England
DATE: June 25, 1994

Did Melanie Roberts' deceased father give his daughter a helping hand of support on the day she was welcomed into the Catholic Church? Look at the veil on her left side and you will see what looks like a hand wearing a ring. Mrs. Jean Roberts, Melanie's mother, sent this photograph to the Society for Psychical Research on November 13, 1994, saying: 'The children had just made their first Holy Communion. Keith's dad took a series of photos. On this one at the side of Melanie is a hand with a ring. No one [underlined twice] else was on the altar at the time. The hand is on the negative. A professional photographer has looked at the photo and negative and cannot explain…'

In fact, no one has been able to explain this image. I definitely discount fraud because there would be no motive for doing such a thing, and a double exposure would not be possible in this case. The likelihood of someone standing behind the girl, perhaps to adjust her headdress or veil, can also be thrown out, because he or she would be very tightly squashed against the rail around the altar and would have disturbed the children. Perhaps part of the same wooden rail has been somehow distorted by the girl's veil? As always, developing chemicals can cause glitches in negatives and prints, but these are usually blurs rather than such a comparatively well defined image. So that takes us back to a proud father on the day of his daughter's first Communion…doesn't it?

'at the side of Melanie is a hand with a ring'

Spirit Head Joins Party Table

LOCATION: Hotel Vierjahreszeiten, Maurach, Austria
DATE: 1988

Psychical researcher Maurice Grosse is adamant about this disturbing photograph, saying, '…fraud can be completely ruled out. The circumstances under which the photograph was taken would not have lent itself to the necessary technical set up to obtain such a picture, even indeed if it was possible at all.' So, who is the oversized woman, with just her head and shoulders on the table? How did she get there? No one yet knows. But here is what was said to have happened. On the last night of a group vacation, four couples met for a farewell party and were joined by three other people. Mr. Todd set up his camera (Canon T50 with Fuji 100 colour film) on a nearby table using a delayed-action ten-second timer and returned to his seat. The shutter clicked and the film wound on, but the flash did not operate (see near right). He reset the camera and took another shot with the flash. No one took much notice when the pictures were developed until one of the subjects, suddenly noticed the outsized head (see top right). The photographic department of Leicester University did not believe it to be a double exposure, and neither did the Society for Psychical Research nor the Royal Photographic Society. Despite the photograph having received publicity nobody has claimed to be the face in the picture. It's said to remain a mystery. Certainly one mystery is why the group of women on the right seemed to have moved seats, so the head conceals none of them. But if this was a deliberate double exposure, how was the 'ghost' woman so precisely placed between the other heads in the group?

> 'who is the oversized woman, with just her head and shoulders on the table?'

The Spectre at the Organ

LOCATION: Unknown
DATE: 1939

Any fan of horror movies knows there is quite a tradition of spooky organ music being heard when no one else is supposed to be around to play it. This is one of the very few photographs known of an actual 'spectral' player, and its story includes some of the best-known followers of Spiritualism from the first half of the 20th century. Mrs. Bertha Harris was well known as a medium in Spiritualist circles, and Lady Conan Doyle introduced her to the psychic photographer William Hope. Mrs. Harris told the psychic researcher, Cyril Permutt, she obtained the best psychic photographs (of spirits who appeared while she was in a séance) if a man and a woman worked together. So Mrs. Harris and Mr. Hope teamed up and the results were splendid. It is not known where they obtained the picture, although the organ looks of a size that would only be found in a church or a hall. With the involvement of Lady Conan Doyle and by inference Sir Arthur, it's difficult to believe the creator of Sherlock Holmes' fanatically forensic mind could be tricked.

Yet the spirit photographs of William Hope have been widely discredited and an association with Mrs. Harris, clearly raises the possibility of collaboration and deceit, perhaps as simple as double exposures. But, just because it is possible to fake photographs of this kind it should not be thought every example is fraudulent. This could be a genuine photograph of a ghostly organist. Couldn't it?

'an actual "spectural" player, and its story includes some of the best followers of spiritualism'

Headless Torso on the Dee

LOCATION: River Dee, Chester, Cheshire, England
DATE: 1994

First you must discount the name of the showboat; in 1994 Diana, Princess of Wales, was still alive and so there's no clue or message from her spirit here. The *Lady Diana* showboat was at its mooring when Mr. and Mrs. Lavender took a snap of her, during a day trip to Chester. When they had the prints developed they were surprised to see the seemingly headless torso and it was duly printed in the *Liverpool Daily Post* on August 17, 1994. Some explanations offered are that the head of the person could simply be bent forward looking at something, that the torso was later superimposed, and that it might simply be a tailor's dummy.

'is it not curious that no one else who was around ever came forward'

These explanations all have flaws. The bend of the neck would have been unnaturally acute to achieve this effect and superimposition of this quality could only have been achieved with computer technology not widely available in 1994. Anyway, the Lavenders claimed neither knowledge nor equipment. That leaves the dummy. Perhaps this is what it was and the Lavenders either have or have not known all the time? But is it not curious that no one else who was around ever came forward to say they saw it too? Then there's the puzzle of which way the headless body is facing. It's generally been thought of as a man, facing away. However, there is also the possibility that the figure is that of a woman. Perhaps the clue is in the showboat after all, and the torso is a theatrical prop put there to have some fun. If so, I wish someone would get in touch and tell me.

Black Figure in Covent Garden

LOCATION: Covent Garden Piazza, London, England
DATE: December 31, 1989

Mr. Webb took this picture of his family, framing his daughter in the foreground and with Mrs. Webb following behind with the push-chair. The legless apparition floating through the scene was not intended to be part of this family group. The couple sent the photograph to the Society for Psychical Research in January 1990. Mrs. Webb says there was no one next to them, that the barrier and the white car made it very difficult for anyone to have passed by them, and also pointed out that there appeared to be an unnatural slant to the strange figure.

'well known for wearing black because she claimed it made her stronger'

Dr. Vernon Harrison, photographic expert of the Society for Psychical Research said 'The whole disposition of the figure seems an impossible one to me for a person in the act of running across the front of the push chair and the dreamy expression on her face does not seem consonant with physical exertion.' He also suggested thoughtography as a possible explanation. After the photograph was published in *Unexplained Magazine* Maurice Grosse (Society for Psychical Research) received a letter from a security guard who used to work at Covent Garden. He said he recognized the girl, explaining she was well known for wearing black because she claimed it made her stronger and that she dabbled in black magic. Grosse replied but did not receive a response. Take another, cool look. Isn't the 'unnatural slant' of the girl just the involuntary head dip we make when we suddenly find ourself in someone else's camera shot? That certainly makes it possible her legs are behind the post. And isn't her dreamy expression the perfectly common 'I'm not impressed' face-set of the young? Up to you.

A Gnarled Hand at her Throat

LOCATION: Essex or Sussex, England
DATE: 1991

Whose is the gnarled hand that intrudes on this picture of three schoolfriends? Kelley Jackson was 12 at the time and says that when she took this picture there was no one else present and no one noticed anything strange. It was three years later in 1994 that she wrote to the Society for Psychical Research: 'We found the hand had arthritic fingers and it couldn't have been anybody from our school because our uniform is red and the sleeve is blue.' That's a puzzling thing to say about an aged adult who surely wouldn't wear the same colour as the pupils and who could also have been someone employed at the castle. Kelley first described the location as 'a castle in Sussex', but later on in her letter she called it 'Mountfiget Castle' [sic]. If she meant 'Mountfichet' castle, this is in Stansted, Essex and not in Sussex.

> 'it couldn't have been anybody from our school'

This is a troubling image but it contains some illogicalities. When I look carefully at the photograph it becomes clear to me the expression of the girl with the hand at her throat is different from the others. Her two companions are smiling but she is gritting her teeth, exactly as you would if someone suddenly laid a hand on you, even in passing, and she is, perhaps, starting to protest. I don't think it important that Kelley is confused about which castle she was in. Castle names aren't very important when you are 12 or 15 years old. But many much older photographers and their subjects famously don't notice or remember fleeting events or changes that are then recorded on their film. I think Kelley and her friends were having such a good time they simply didn't notice what really did happen. If there is not such a rational explanation then this becomes a very real anomaly, and one that is certainly worth exploring in much greater depth.

Execution on the Underground

LOCATION: Bakerloo Line Underground train, London, England
DATE: 1985

Why would Bruno Richard Hauptmann, executed for the kidnap and murder of the Lindbergh baby in 1936, appear in the window of a London Underground train? That's what Mrs. Woo needed to know. She thought she had simply taken a snap of her nephew from Malaysia, who badly wanted a picture of himself on the Underground. Yet when the picture was developed, there seemed to be the partial picture of a man in an electric chair with sparks coming from his hands, just above her nephew's head. For some reason, Mrs. Woo recognized the likeness as similar to the waxwork in Madame Tussaud's famous 'Chamber of Horrors'. Sure enough, the waxwork was identical (minus the sparks), but there were no posters advertising the museum at the time, and anyway, the picture was taken between stations, so a poster visible through the window can be discounted. Subsequently a medium confirmed it was Hauptmann that Mrs. Woo had captured, and claimed he was saying he was innocent of the crime for which he had been executed.

> **'he was saying he was innocent of the crime for which he had been executed'**

The lighting of this photograph is curiously shallow, with no apparent flash reflection in the window or details of the seats in which they are sitting, not even between their clearly lit legs. Mrs. Woo's obvious belief in the paranormal means thoughtography could be a plausible explanation for this real conundrum. I have to say, though, that a plausible explanation of any kind for this picture, including a paranormal one, remains intriguingly unknown.

Apparition at Arundel Altar

LOCATION: St. Nicholas' Church, Arundel, Sussex, England
DATE: 1940

A ghostly vigil at the altar or a photographic error? What gives away a double exposure, whether intended or not, is faint remainders of other parts of the second picture, surrounding the main subject. This type of occurence seems especially likely at a time of such little photographic sophistication as World War II. Could there really have been a carved white structure stuck so tightly between the right-hand pews and the altar rail? Are they part of the emanation, or clues to trick photography? In 1989 computer enhancement was alleged to have found the picture was probably 'a multiple exposure of a woman ascending the altar steps with a taper and lighting one of the altar candles'. This makes sense for paranormal sceptics, but less sense for photography sceptics. Did anyone really have such good computers in 1989?

This church in the grounds of Arundel Castle was built on the site of a Norman priory, and the adjoining Fitzalan Chapel, originally part of the same church, also has a tradition of being haunted. Ghosts are commonly seen in places where emotions can be extreme. It thus makes sense to learn pubs are a frequent place for paranormal sightings. So churches, where everything from baptisms to weddings and funerals are held, are prime sites. This is a classic ghost picture exactly where you expect to see one. Is this why it is suspicious, or does that make it curiously reassuring?

'Ghosts are commonly seen in places where emotions can be extreme'

The Uninvited Guest

LOCATION: Zoetermeer, Holland
DATE: 1994?

There is a rather distinct mystery about the ephemeral image seen in both these photographs sent to the Society for Psychical Research. Uncommonly, there are more than just two photographs known, and they have each been taken from dramatically different points of view. Thus, because the unidentified phenomenon is seen so diversely, there seems no possibility of it being a curiosity of light or of it being a camera fault. The number of images and range of viewpoints, which must have been taken over a period of time, make highly unusual circumstances and create one of the most intriguing cases of all. The same person was said to have taken both these pictures, using the same camera. No one else in the church appeared to be aware of the apparition, as you can see for yourself.

On the right of the altar there is certainly a shape. It might be thought human, perhaps with an outstretched arm and head covering. What do you think it is? One explanation could be pareidolia, the self-protective trait of the human brain, which translates unknown shapes into something familiar, to calm our fears. Rise above this and refuse to see something recognizable if you want, but then you have to ask yourself what it might be if not once a human being; there is no rule to say what a ghost should look like. It would be fascinating to track down the bride and groom and ask if either had a close, but dead, relative whom they wished had been at the wedding. Or whom they had dreaded being at the wedding, yet who unexpectedly turned up.

'there seems no possibility of it being a curiosity of light'

The Spirit of Old Nanna

LOCATION: Unknown
DATE: 1991

Two-year-old Greg Sheldon Maxwell is obviously entranced by something he can see. These moments of rapture happened whenever he began pointing to part of a room and saying, 'Old Nanna's here'. But Old Nanna, his great grandmother, was dead, and no one else could see a thing. The boy's moments of classic transfixion were then photographed with the result you can see, but the mist was only revealed on the print; again no one else in the room saw anything.

The story sort of makes sense paranormally, yet there is not enough verifiable fact to support the appearance and photographing of a spirit. We don't know who the photographer was, or what was shown in any other pictures taken. Did the boy often sit with his fingers folded together, as children do when they first learn to pray, or only when he was experiencing something wonderful? If the picture is fraudulent then the misty cloud should be explainable but it's far too big and dense to be, say, cigarette smoke. Neither is there anything to suggest a human form but, of course, what the boy saw and what we are permitted to see could be quite different.

'moments of rapture happened whenever he began pointing to part of a room and saying "Old Nanna's here"'

The Forgotten Prisoner of Newgate

LOCATION: Old Newgate Prison, City of London, England
DATE: 1988

Newgate Prison in the City of London was infamous, the most feared lock-up in all England for almost one thousand years. Until 1868 condemned men and women were hung outside its walls, while the public watched, and from then until 1901 the hangings took place inside. Today, The Old Bailey, England's premier courts of justice, stands on the site. But, beneath the ground, some of the cells still exist, cells where starving, neglected men, women, and children lived in unspeakable misery. In 1988 Lars Thomas was on a guided tour of the basement of the Viaduct Inn, built over some of these former cells. He was certain no one stood in front of him when he took the picture but as you can see, someone or something did manifest itself, with a head craned up as though looking for an ever-impossible escape.

> 'beneath the ground, some of the cells still exist, cells where starving, neglected men, women and children lived in unspeakable misery'

Using daylight film when the lighting was from tungsten-filament bulbs causes the curious red tone of the photograph. This is a common occurrence familiar to most photographers. So that's not mysterious. What has to be considered is if this unexpected image really is, or once was, a man. Is the neck puzzlingly too thin, and is that a bald head or a flat cap? Those answers might be there if the image were less blurred. That's if there is an answer. No use saying, 'If these walls could speak…' Perhaps they have spirits among them anxious to be seen and to speak?

FAMOUS MYSTERIES

If just one of these mysterious shots genuinely shows someone or something from outside current understanding, the scientific world would have to change or adapt many of its long-held theories. And so would we. That's why these images are so very famous internationally.

Some of these photographs have been being analyzed for more than a century. Each one still prompts discussion, sometimes heated, for and against its validity. Suggestions that the image caught by security cameras at Belgrave Hall is simply an out-of-focus oak leaf seem plausible. But this was caught on videotape, and there is no sign of the 'leaf' coming into or out of the frame. Whatever it is just appears, remains for a few seconds, and then disappears. That's why it's still being talked about in the committees of the psychical research societies. Examples from the USA and Australia are particularly interesting because they take us away from the suspicious settings of the ivy-clad country houses, old churches, and ruined castles of England. Yet, if the paranormal is a reality it must be seen in every country, and rather than being surprised to find the photograph taken in a graveyard of Chicago, we should be comforted. If, that is, we believe in the paranormal.

Of course, one needs to accept the testimony of the photographers as a starting point and hope they are not either lying outright or being economical with the truth. Does someone know the living identity of the woman on the tombstone in Bachelor's Grove, Chicago? Does someone know the technical secrets of the triple shot of the boy without a shirt? The Tulip Staircase, taken by Canadians at Greenwich, London, has probably appeared in more books than any other, and still hasn't been satisfactorily explained. It, like others you will see, shows a particular image of an apparition, in ghostly white drapery. But we still don't know for sure what we are seeing.

As you will have realized by now, there have been 'ghost' photographs claimed since the beginnings of photography. Hundreds have been sent to psychical researchers over the years, most of which are easily explainable.

But others are not. In recent years the advent of digital cameras, cameras on mobile phones, the ease of photo-manipulation and the internet have vastly proliferated the number of anomalous photographs that crop up, but also make it harder to believe that they are genuine. It's all too easy to assume that some sort of digital manipulation has taken place. The photographs in this chapter have stood up to scrutiny. They have been published repeatedly, investigated by psychical researchers, and yet still haven't given up their secrets.

White Lady on the Tombstone

LOCATION: Bachelor's Grove Cemetery, Chicago, Illinois, USA
DATE: August 10, 1991

Some people believe the White Lady of Bachelor's Grove is the ghost of Mrs. Rogers, searching mournfully for the grave of her dead baby or sitting in communion with its spirit. An unnamed infant is buried close by. This image by Mari Huff was taken near the south entrance of the graveyard and shows a saddened, somewhat slumped woman, sitting on the well known tombstone with a checkered pattern carved into it. The strange white mist around her feet is said to be the natural debris of leaves, grass and twigs affected by the type of film used.

'searching mournfully for the grave of her dead baby'

There is a long tradition of apparitions, strange blue orbs, and other paranormal phenomena in this graveyard, and it was the site of a tragic murder. In 1991 the Ghost Research Society mounted a vigil, using black and white infrared film to photograph the location. The Society states very clearly that no one was in the shot when it was taken. Even if someone did get into the photo and rested there for a while, it's hard to explain why the far leg is so transparent and the face is so shapeless. One notion is that the face has been tampered with and the leg was moved into that position during the exposure, thus not allowing the film to fix it accurately. But once again, cool reasoning must be used. Why would the Society fiddle with or lie about a subject they take so seriously?

Did Freddy Jackson Return?

LOCATION: Probably HMS *Daedalus*, Lee-on-Solent, Hampshire, England
DATE: 1919

Did air-mechanic Freddy Jackson return from the dead to be in this photograph? In 1919 the Royal Naval Air Service, later the Fleet Air Arm, was established at Lee-on-Solent, now RAF Cranwell. Probably serving on HMS *Daedalus*, this photograph of fellow airmen from his squadron was taken two days after a plane's propeller killed Freddy. Look closely behind the left ear of the fourth airman from the left, on the top row. The close-up clearly shows another man's face, and many of his friends are said to have recognized it as Freddy. Spookily, the picture was taken on the same day as his funeral; perhaps Freddy didn't know he was dead, and turned up for the photograph as arranged.

'taken on the same day as his funeral; perhaps Freddy didn't know he was dead'

Sir Victor Goddard, a retired RAF officer who was present brought the picture to public attention first, but this was not until 1975, more than half a century after it was taken. A number of other sources have published it subsequently, but none provides concrete evidence about how the 'extra' image was identified, or by whom. This is a typical case where the explanation might not be something paranormal. It may simply be another man making an appearance during the exposure, or one of the airman moving. But it does appear to be a different face to the man from behind whom he is peering – and unlike everyone else in the picture, he doesn't appear to be wearing a cap. An interesting photograph worthy of inclusion in a collection of this type. Not least because it might jog the memory of similar photographs from other private collections that are waiting to be examined and explained.

The Girl Who Returned

LOCATION: Town Hall, Wem, Shropshire, England
DATE: November 19, 1995

Is this Jane Churm, accused of burning down the Wem Town Hall in 1677? This seems to be one paranormal explanation for this extraordinarily dramatic photograph. Tony O'Rahilly took the shot as Wem Town Hall was being gutted by a fire. Because of the intense heat, police and firemen had stopped people getting close to the flames. This meant he had to photograph the building from the other side of the road, using a 200mm telescopic lens. Nobody remembers seeing anyone in the blaze, which was so intense that survival would not have been possible. The face has never been formally identified, so who is she, and what is this girl in the old-fashioned bonnet trying to communicate to us today?

'was she still frantically trying to communicate something?'

The photograph was sent to the Association for the Scientific Study of Anomalous Phenomena, who in turn sent it to the photographic expert, Dr. Vernon Harrison. He declared that neither the picture nor the negative had been doctored, but that it might have been produced by a trick of light causing an optical illusion. Some of the architectural details need explaining, but it's an arresting combination. A pretty girl and two fires on the same historic site: just the sort of dramatic coincidence you might expect in a Hollywood thriller. Or, it could be true that Jane Churm did return on the night the Town Hall burned down again. Was she still frantically trying to communicate something about the original blaze, almost 320 years earlier?

Manifestation in a Security Camera

LOCATION: Belgrave Hall Museum, Leicester, England
DATE: December 23, 1998

At 4:48 am precisely this spectral image suddenly appeared on a security camera outside Belgrave Hall Museum. It remained still for five seconds and then instantly disappeared without any blurring of fall or flight. At the same time there was a digital timing malfunction, as though time was being suddenly displaced. Yet mechanical failure can be ruled out. This was a new security system, tested only one month earlier and subsequently retested. The site of the alleged apparition is especially relevant, because the 18th-century hall is supposedly built on crossroads used as an unhallowed graveyard for those not welcome in consecrated ground. And there had long been claims of a ghostly figure appearing inside the hall as well as scary sounds and untraceable smells.

In 1999 the press took up the possibility of a Belgrave Hall haunting, and explanations generated included the spirit of a Victorian lady, a plastic bag, a blown leaf, insects, and raindrops on the lens of the camera, but there was no rain and no strong wind on the night. The Association for the Scientific Study of Anomalous Phenomena undertook two vigils there without reporting any unusual phenomena. They also tried to replicate the image by using leaves thrown into the air. To them and to the museum staff this appeared to be the most likely explanation. But they had not considered the digital timing malfunction and Maurice Grosse of the Society for Psychical Research said he was convinced 'the security camera captured a manifestation of psychic activity'. No truly convincing explanation has ever been given.

'the 18th-century hall is supposedly built on crossroads used as an unhallowed graveyard'

The Observer at Corroboree Rock

LOCATION: Corroboree Rock, Alice Springs, Northern Territory, Australia
DATE: 1959

Few occasions can be more sacred or spiritual than an Aboriginal corroboree, when rhythmic percussion, didgeridoo music, traditional songs, and repetitive dancing create tribal unity under night skies. Corroboree Rock is 100 miles west of Alice Springs and the chosen site for other important rites. There is little familiar about the figure, who seems to be dressed in an all-encasing robe and tight-fitting helmet, not what you would normally choose in the stifling temperatures at the very heart of Australia.

'a bizarre solution other than the paranormal occurs to me'

Even more puzzling is what he is holding and looking at so intently. Some sort of camera perhaps? This is one case where a bizarre solution other than the paranormal occurs to me. Is this someone from another planet, who allowed himself to be seen? If it is simply an unidentified human, the unique photographs he took that day have have never been seen. So, who or what was the silent observer at Corroboree Rock? Contentiously, I should add that a church minister took this shot, it is usual to think a minister is above suspicion when providing details of the paranormal, but it is naïve to believe that every case reported has been without inaccuracies, intentional or otherwise.

Who is the Back Seat Passenger?

LOCATION: Ipswich, Suffolk, England
DATE: March 22, 1959

Mabel Chinnery and her husband had just visited her mother's grave. She decided to use the last shot in her camera to photograph her husband sitting alone in the car. Mrs. Chinnery was convinced the developed image showed another figure, her dead mother, with light reflected in her spectacles, sitting in her favourite spot in the car. No one should doubt her sincerity but perhaps she put a human face on to something unfamiliar and otherwise unsettling.

'Powerful emotions could have let Mrs. Chainey create a thought photograph of her departed mother'

In this case, the possibility of a double exposure must be considered. On the right is what at first seems to be the door pillar of the far side of the car, but isn't it much too far forward, aren't the windows too big, and does the curved right side looks like a tree trunk? The supposed mother's figure looks unnaturally close to the front seat and couldn't be sitting on the back seat. Even Mr. Chinnery's face seems too big. Was the window open or closed? Before this can be accepted as a genuine paranormal image, these points have to be rationalized. Until then it's just as likely Mrs. Chinnery's emotional state confused her about the her last shot, famously easy to expose twice. Yet many believe the same powerful emotions could have let Mrs. Chinnery create a thought photograph of her departed mother, and that other unexplained phenomena are simply a result of this imagery from another realm. This would then be an extraordinary example of an unidentified power of the human mind.

Apparition at Hampton Court Palace

LOCATION: Hampton Court Palace, Middlesex, England
DATE: October 7, 2003

Security staff heard alarms, activated by fire doors, which should always have been kept closed. They checked the CCTV footage to find out what had happened and were astonished to see this skeletal figure in a long, hooded cloak emerge from behind the doors. Romantic, redbrick Hampton Court Palace appears to sit serenely by the gentle Thames River. But its history is violent, the scene of much turbulence, betrayal, and death. No wonder there are tales of more than one royal haunting: the most likely candidates would be two of Henry VIII's wives; Anne Boleyn executed in 1536 or Catherine Howard, beheaded in 1542. Even Henry himself is supposed to have been seen, as well as a sad pageboy from the time of Charles II.

> '**No wonder there are tales of more than one royal haunting**'

There's absolutely no denying the presence of a figure and that the clothing seems authentically historical. To me it looks more like a determined man than the spirit of a restless queen of Tudor England. The sceptical Richard Wiseman, professor of psychology, University of Hertfordshire, says that if this were a genuine apparition the spectre would be a 'significant discovery'. He's more likely to go along with those who say it was a tourist in a costume who was lost, or a member of staff who dressed up to do this, for publicity's sake. But the testimony of all the palace staff denies this and they stress that these doors are in a part of the building off limits to the public. Neither has been identified, if that were so. Experiments at the palace have shown genuinely colder areas associated with alleged haunting are actually cooled by drafts from concealed doors. What do you think? Is there always a logical answer, or could this be the genuine image of an apparition on film, one of the most rare things in the world?

Spectre Priest at Woodford Altar

LOCATION: St. Mary the Virgin, Woodford, Northamptonshire, England
DATE: July 1964

Two years after it was taken, Gordon Carroll and his friend David Hadsell were astonished to find that this photograph included the image of what looks like someone in deep meditation before the altar of St. Mary the Virgin's church. This is not seen in the next frame he took. Gordon was only 16 at the time, but took great care about his photographs, using a tripod for this shot to eliminate any camera shake.

> 'a fleeting spectral instance, usually hidden from our sight'

It's very easy for sceptics to claim a cleaner might have been at work or that a passing vicar might have knelt there briefly, although a short-sleeved white shift tied at the waist seems unlikely clerical attire. Gordon and David were both convinced no one had approached the altar while they were taking photographs, and two heads are much more believable than one. To support their veracity and honesty the local vicar gave them both a pristine character reference and Agfa (the film manufacturers) said there were no traces of a double exposure, and 'no flaw in the actual film or fault in development'.

But there is a very plausible explanation, if you believe in the paranormal. St. Mary the Virgin's former priest, the Reverend Basil Eversley Owen, had died only the year before and he was well known for spending time in devotion on this very spot. You can only speculate about whether he had returned, or if he had never left and the teenagers captured a fleeting spectral instance, usually hidden from our sight.

The Haunted Doorway

LOCATION: Probably England
DATE: 1920s

This is the classic image of what most people would think a ghost should look like, a semi-transparent shrouded figure. Hollywood has certainly done everything in its power to reinforce such expectations. This photograph is generally known among those interested in the paranormal as Spencer's Ghost, but only because it was sent to psychical researcher John Spencer, some time in 1993. Spencer was sufficiently intrigued by the picture to investigate and even consulted a medium, who suggested the thatched building (more a barn than a cottage, perhaps) might be in a village near Mottram, Greater Manchester. Spencer added: 'While a number of methods could be suggested for faking the "ghost", inquiries made of various photographers suggest that whatever the apparition might or might not be it was genuinely in front of the camera when the photograph was taken. The mystery still remains.'

The dearth of information means the authenticity of this photograph will always be dubious, not least because most people are suspicious of the dramatic drapery, when by far the majority of investigations of the Society for Psychical Research have been sightings of what looked like real people in real clothes. Modern computers are constant proof of how much a photograph can lie, but they can also prove the reverse. One day, technology could well tell us this apparition is exactly what it seems to be: a genuine paranormal presence.

'it was genuinely in front of the camera when the photograph was taken'

Triple Echo of the Future

LOCATION: Virginia, USA
DATE: 1950s

Accidental triple exposures are virtually unheard of, but such a rarity is an outside possibility here. The stories that come with this startling picture certainly make you think something else might have happened. Sam Watkins thought he was taking a picture of his dog, but when he developed the Polaroid print he found three ghostly images of his brother instead. What's more, just a few days later, a passing car hit his brother and he was dressed exactly like this when it happened.

'just a few days later a passing car hit his brother'

Polaroid cameras were notorious for taking double-exposures if you accidentally pressed the button twice in quick enough succession. Yet, look again at the boy who was allegedly involved in a car accident a few days later. None of the images are noticeably sharper than the others and with multi-exposures the first one or the last one is usually clearer. And what's going on with the shadows? The two on the left go one way, and the one on the right goes the other. A slippage of time might be thought to have caused this anomaly and to be a warning of tragedy to come. Often, the anomalous explanation is easier to accept. Until I see and hear an explanation of how a triple image could have been faked on a Polaroid, my mind is open, but leaning towards a paranormal occurrence.

Spooky Giant at the Altar

LOCATION: Church of Christ the Consoler, Skelton-cum-Newby, Yorkshire, England
DATE: July or August 1954

When a respectable vicar says he took a photograph like this in his own church, you have to at least accept that he thinks he's telling the truth. The Reverend Kenneth F. Lord said it was a summer evening, about 6 pm, and that no one else was in the church except for a single friend. That abnormally tall figure on the steps to the altar is certainly not the friend he's talking about! His purpose was to photograph the altar and not until the film was developed did he notice this curious ghoul.

Even if you accept the possibility of accidental but somehow overlooked or forgotten double exposure, you have to ask why a vicar would choose to photograph someone dressed like they were wearing a Hallowe'en spook costume, and at the wrong time of year. The mask looks like sheeting rather than something vaporous and spiritual. And on second look, the apparition might not be as tall as first appears, but could be standing on the top step, the robe artfully draped and arranged over the other two. This is clearly not what you would expect from something supposedly without substance. But as I've asked before, what should a ghost look like? If this is as genuine a photograph as the Reverend Lord believes, it is truly one of the most remarkable examples of an apparition ever recorded.

'one of the most remarkable examples of an apparition ever recorded'

The Tulip Staircase Mystery

LOCATION: The Queen's House, Greenwich, London, England
DATE: June 19, 1966

The Tulip Staircase was barred to visitors so the Reverend and Mrs. Hardy from Canada took a photograph to study later. They had come especially to learn more about the exquisite architectural details of The Queen's House in Greenwich. Queen Anne commissioned it in the height of 1616 fashion from the architect Inigo Jones. It was her escape from the general disinterest in her by her husband, King James I of England and VI of Scotland. The staircase was entrancing, unique for its beautiful tulip motifs on the curved flight up to the next floor, and they were thrilled they at least had a photograph. But they got more than they expected, for the print showed the straining image of someone in grey robes, perhaps a monk, clinging to the balustrade, and seeming to want to drag itself up the staircase. But to what?

A thorough appraisal of the photograph was made, including interviews of the Hardys who confirmed nobody else was on the stairs. A Ghost Club vigil produced no conclusive evidence of a haunting despite inexplicable sounds and impressions being noted. The National Maritime Museum's photographer Brian Tremain did replicate a similar photograph using a member of staff on the staircase and a long exposure. But his success does not mean the Hardys were hoaxers; there is every reason to believe a man of the cloth and his wife about something so fundamental to their personal belief as spirits. So, we are left with a dilemma. Who or what was trying to ascend the Tulip Staircase and why did it choose to appear only to the Reverend and Mrs. Hardy? It's a mystery we may never solve.

'the print showed
the straining
image of someone
in grey robes'

GHOSTS IN THE HOUSE

It seems that most ghost pictures are taken by happenstance. A picture is snapped and lo and behold, strange figures show up in the photo! Interestingly enough, most people don't even notice the ghost images in their photos until they begin to look for them. So, if you fancy the life of a ghost hunter, start by checking through your photo albums.

If you happen to have a ghost in your house, you are not alone. Do your keys regularly disappear only to be discovered somewhere other than where you left them? Maybe you aren't losing your mind after all. Keep an eye out for the tell-tale signs of a haunting; some of these may seem insignificant and can easily be overlooked, but if more than a few of these ring a bell with you, you may have an uninvited guest in your home.

Signs of a haunting
1. Feeling of being watched.
2. Voices out of nowhere.
3. The sound of footsteps.
4. Household objects mysteriously disappearing only to be found elsewhere.
5. The phone ringing, but no one is there when it is answered.

6. Strange odours that have no source.
7. Lights or appliances being turned on or off.
8. Animals acting strangely.
9. Books or other objects being thrown off shelves.
10. Cold spots.
11. Feeling of being touched.
12. Appearance of a transparent being.
13. Feeling of sadness.
14. Strange shadows.
15. Cabinets opening and closing.

How does one get rid of a ghost in their house? It depends on the haunting, the type of ghost or entity, and why it's there. Those who believe they may be haunted would be advised to contact a local group of ghost hunters or investigators to see what they can recommend.

The photos offered in this chapter are fascinating but be warned, you may end up sleeping with the lights on afterwards.

Uninvited Guest at Lodge

This extraordinary photograph of what appears to be a shadow ghost at a curtained window was taken in August 2004 at the Comstock Lodge in Virginia City, Nevada, USA by hotel guest Raul Juarez. There was no one else in his room when Raul took this photograph and he cannot find an explanation for the photographic anomaly. There is nothing in the room that could have cast such a shadow as this and, even more puzzling, there is no reflection of the shadowy figure in the mirror.

In the lightened photograph below you can see that the image resembles the shape of a man and you can detect a hat – a stereotypical trait of shadow beings. Ghost investigators state that Virginia City is notorious for being one of the most common places to experience the supernatural. Considering the photograph's integrity, location and detail, we can only assume that Raul was not alone in his room, as he had originally thought.

'We can only assume that Raul was not alone in the room, as he had originally thought...'

Shadow Ghost Grabs Child

Adam was browsing through his latest batch of developed family photographs when he came upon this terrifying image of what appears to be a shadow ghost grabbing hold of his young nephew. Understandably Adam feared for the little boy.

There have been several accounts of people being menaced and chased by shadow beings, but rarely attacked. It is incredible, therefore, to have an extraordinarily defined photograph of such an event. Closer inspection of this incredible photograph reveals that there may be even more to the story. Look to the left of the picture, at the boy's arm and shoulder. Can you see a white hand? And, just above the hand, is that a glimpse of a white face? Is there an attempt underway to rescue the boy from his shadow-being abductor? Could this be a case of good vs. evil? Happily on this occasion the shadow being was thwarted and we can report that the boy is safe and well.

'Could this be a case of good vs. evil?...'

Girl in the Door

This picture was taken after setting up a QuickCam on a new family computer. The owner of the picture claims that he was testing the camera by taking a few photographs, but he did not notice the image of the girl until two weeks later when he was going through the picture files. It looks as though a child is walking directly through the solid door.

Webcams like the QuickCam are becoming quite useful in the ghost hunting community. Ghost hunters set them up in a haunted location in the hope of catching an elusive ghost on film. This footage can also be shared with ghost enthusiasts online. But cam operators have to be careful not to make the mistake of identifying motion blur – caused when someone runs or walks quickly past the camera – as the presence of a ghost. However this image does not exhibit the classic characteristics of motion blur (see page 154). Could the fact that a friend of the family passed away the night that this photo was taken provide an answer to why an apparition of a young girl should appear from nowhere?

'It looks as though a child is walking directly through the solid door...'

The Green Family Ghost

This old photograph of the Green family was being scanned by Josh for his online family tree, when he noticed something very unusual about it. The scanned image revealed that a white-hooded woman watching from the screen door was also posing for the camera that day.

Some might dismiss the ghostly figure as a classic example of double exposure, and yet if this were the case it is unlikely that the apparition would be so perfectly contained within the window frame. The lack of detail in the figure's face suggests that this is indeed a spectral apparition rather than a living person. Of course, we cannot completely rule out glare or reflection as the cause of the anomaly, but isn't it just possible that a deceased family member decided to show up for the photo call?

'a white-hooded woman watching from the screen door was also posing for the camera that day...'

Haunted Mirror in the Hall

This picture first emerged at a ghost conference in Virginia City, Nevada, USA in 2002. Tony claimed that he had a haunted house that was especially active, and not only that, he also had the photographic evidence to prove it. Tony told onlookers that he had taken the picture of his hallway mirror whilst attempting to gather visual evidence of his hauntings. He was adamant that he was standing alone in the hallway.

The photo certainly seems to back up Tony's allegations that he had been haunted, however a reflection in the mirror – especially when cameras are involved – could also be a valid explanation for this figure. Although it could quite possibly be a dark entity of sorts, we still can't completely rule out a distorted reflection of Tony.

'He was adamant that he was standing alone in the hallway...'

Lady of the Mansion

In 2005 this picture was taken at the Bard Mansion on the Port Hueneme Naval Base in Ventura County, California, USA with an Olympus Stylus 4.0 megapixel camera. Thomas R. Bard was a California Senator from 1900–1905 and it is claimed that this is the apparition of Bard's wife. The second picture is of a close up of the apparition, which has been lightened.

Not everyone would agree that this is an authentic ghost photo and a true ghost hunter should never accept an image on face value. Do your own research and consider the integrity of the photographer and their transcript of the event. And finally gain an understanding of photography and how photo imaging programs work – the more you know, the better qualified you are to make a decision.

'it is claimed that this is the apparition of the Bard's wife...'

Ghosts on Fire

When Kerry heard that a friend's family home had been involved in a fire, she was just relieved to hear that they were all safe as they had been out watching a softball game at the time. Later when she saw the photos of the incident taken by the local fire department she couldn't believe her eyes. Were spirits trying to escape the flames?

In the burning smoke escaping from the top floor window some see a face of an old man with large staring eyeballs and a wide-open, maybe screaming, mouth. Others see three screaming heads with a tortured and twisted look on their faces. Looking back, the family recalls that there had been strange happenings in their home, and the toddler would often try to communicate with people who weren't there, or stretch out her arms to be picked up by an invisible being. So maybe the ghostly residents of the house were not as lucky as the living ones that day.

'three heads, with a tortured and twisted look on their faces...'

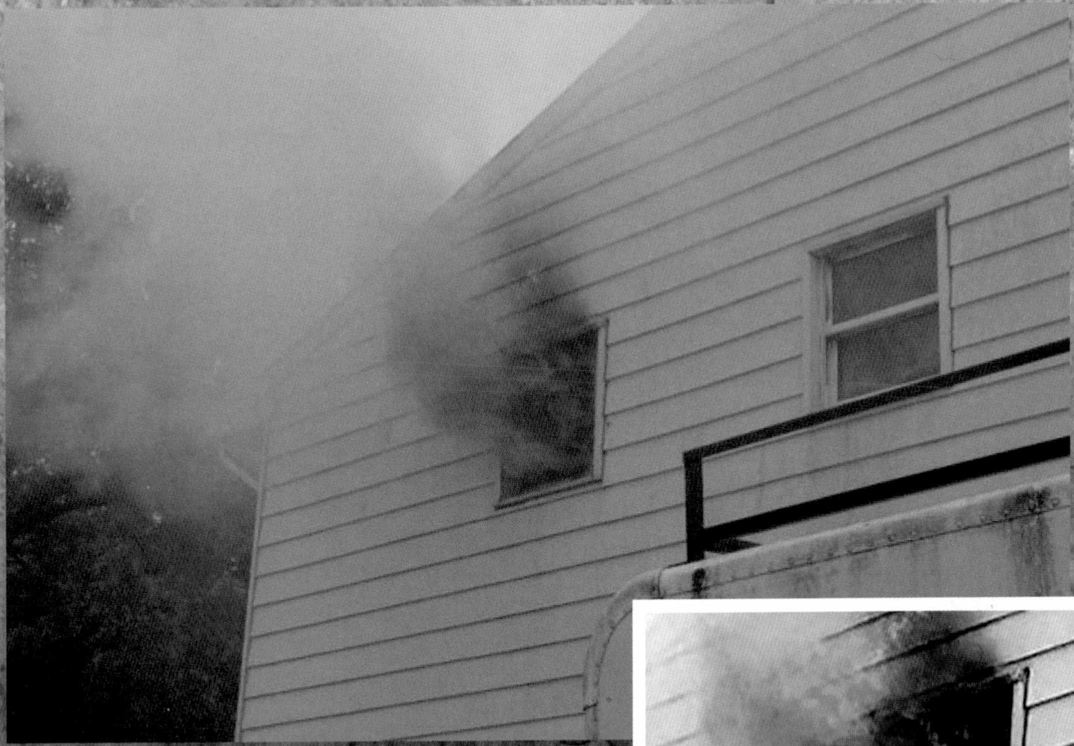

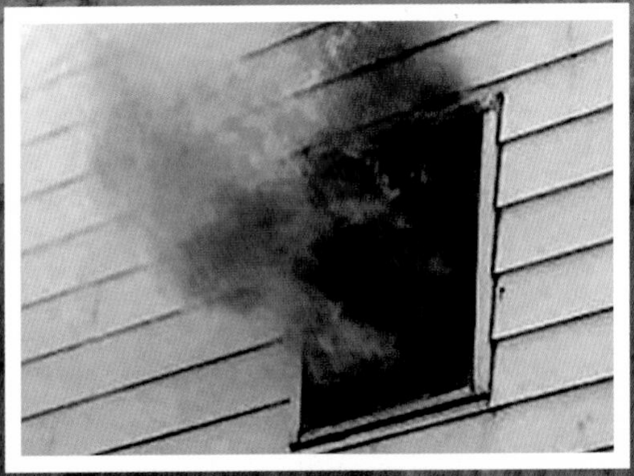

A Cry for Help

This old abandoned house in Lakeland, Florida, USA was the location of a terrible and tragic suicide where a young girl hanged herself many years before. The ghost hunting team that took the picture believes this to be photographic evidence of her lingering tormented soul.

This has all the signs of being a 'soft ghost' – rather than being an optical illusion there is the possibility that it is something paranormal, although it is impossible to say for sure. The ghost hunters' van was parked parallel to the window, so we can establish that its headlights were not directly facing the house and therefore we can discount glare or reflection as a cause of the ghostly image. The team took a few pictures before they fled the area. Did they feel an uncomfortable presence when they parked alongside the house that night, or did the image of the ghostly noose to the right of the picture frighten them away?

'The ghost hunting team...believes this to be photographic evidence of her lingering tormented soul...'

Phantom at the Window

This photo started circulating the web several years ago and has gathered a lot of attention ever since. It shows a rather evil-looking uninvited guest as a family prepares for their three-year-old's birthday party. Family friend Debbie submitted this photograph when she realized that the figure in the window was actually inside the house between the curtains and the window. She was quite alarmed by what she had captured on film, especially as there was no one in the house at the time.

Even if there was someone in the house, surely they wouldn't have looked like this! Although it could be a reflection or that something menacing had been placed in the window of the house, this picture was enough to unsettle not only the family but the thousands who have viewed it since.

'It shows a rather evil-looking uninvited guest...'

And Ghost Makes Three

Sean couldn't believe it when Carol, his girlfriend, showed him this bizarre picture of her aunt and uncle. The photo dates back to September 1980 and it resurfaced after it was found in a sealed envelope in her grandmother's possessions. Carol contacted her aunt and uncle who were oblivious that they had posed for a photograph beside a ghost.

There are several possible explanations for this ghostly effect. It may have been cigarette smoke in front of the lens although this is unlikely because of the amount of detail in the face, shirt, torso, and upper arm. It may also be glare or shadow; an optical illusion; or even photo manipulation. But then again it could truly be a ghost.

'they were oblivious that they had posed for a photograph beside a ghost...'

Night-vision Apparition

Dominic took this picture with a Sony DCR-TRV17 camera with the night vision setting on. This particular camcorder is a favourite among ghost hunters because it was one of the first to have night vision, which allows you to film and take pictures in the dark. Dominic had just recieved the camera and was experimenting with this setting by taking still shots around her house when this glowing image appeared in her bedroom. She claims to have seen it through the LCD screen twice and took a picture the second time that it appeared.

'this glowing image appeared in her bedroom...'

Ghost at the Window

Ashley works for a glazing company and took this picture of a housing-complex for elderly people after her company installed new glass windows there. A strange and menacing figure appeared in the window of the ground floor flat and yet the property was vacant at the time.

Who or what might this be? Given that the windows are newly installed and therefore clean and clear, it is unlikely that this effect has been caused by smudging or glare on the glass. Perhaps a tenant who has passed away is unwilling to move on and is making his presence known from beyond the grave? It certainly invites debate.

'the strange and menacing figure appeared in the window of the ground floor flat...'

Bibliography

Annals Of Psychical Science (London, 1913).

Apraxine, Pierre, Canguilhem, Denis, Chéroux, Clément, Fischer, Andreas and Schmit, Sophie (eds.), *The Perfect Medium: Photography and the Occult* (Yale University Press, 2004).

Baraduc, H., *The Human Soul: Its Movements, Its Lights, and the Iconography Of the Fluid Invisible* (London, 1913).

Barbanell, Maurice, 'Scientist Took 44 Photos of Spirit Form', *Noah's Ark*, 3, 50 (September 1994), 9-12.

The British Journal of Photography (1982/1983).

Carroll, Robert Todd, *The Skeptic's Dictionary*, (John Wiley & Sons, 2003).

Dash, Mike, 'Whatever Happened to Spirit Photography?', *Fortean Times*, 123 (June 1999).

Doyle, Sir Arthur Conan, *The Coming of the Fairies* (Hodder & Stoughton, 1922).

Earwicker, Simon, 'The Witness Camera', *ASSAP News*, 77 (July 2000), 4–5.

Eisenbud, J., *The World of Ted Serios: 'Thoughtographic' Studies of an Extraordinary Mind* (William Morrow Company, 1967).

Fielding, Everard, *Sittings with Eusapia Palladino & Other Studies* (New York University Books, 1963).

Fodor, Nandor, *Encyclopaedia of Psychic Science* (Arthurs Press Limited, London, 1933).

Gettings, Fred, *Ghosts in Photographs: The Extraordinary Story of Spirit Photography* (Outlet, 1978).

Haining, Peter, *Ghosts: The Illustrated History* (Sidgwick & Jackson, London,1974).

Houghton, Georgina, *Chronicles of the Photographs of Spiritual Beings and Phenomena Invisible to the Material Eye Interblended With Personal Narrative* (London, 1882).

Into the Unknown, (Reader's Digest, 1982).

Jones, R., *Walking Haunted London* (New Holland Publishers, London, 1999).
Journal of the Society for Psychical Research, 59, 830 (1993).
Krauss, R., *Beyond Light and Shadow* (Nazraeli Press, Munich, 1994).
Lamar Keene, M. and Spraggett, Allen, *The Psychic Mafia* (Dell Publishing, 1976).
Marriott, William, *Pearson's Magazine* (1910).
McEwan, Graham J., *Haunted Churches of England* (Robert Hale, London, 1989).
Mumler, W. M., *Personal Experiences of William H. Mumler in Spirit Photography* (Colby & Rich, 1875).
Pagan Dawn (The Pagan Federation, London).
Parker, D. and Parker, J., *Atlas of the Supernatural* (Prentice Hall Press, New York, 1990).
Permutt, Cyril, *Beyond the Spectrum* (Patrick Stephens, Cambridge, 1983).
Picknett, Lynn, *The Encyclopaedia of the Paranormal* (Guild Publishing, London, 1990).
Princess Mary, *Princess Mary's Gift Book* (Hodder & Stoughton, London, 1917).
'Proceedings of the Parapsychology Association', 5 (1968).
Randi, James, *The Supernatural A-Z* (Headline Book Publishing, London 1995).
Townsend, Maurice, 'How To Take Anomalous Photos', *Anomaly*, 38 (May 2005), 2–15.
Underwood, Peter, *The Ghost Hunter's Guide* (Javelin Books, London, 1988).
Underwood, Peter, *Ghosts and How To See Them* (BCA, London, 1993).
Underwood, Peter, *Nights in Haunted Houses* (Headline, London, 1994).
Willin, M. J., *Music, Witchcraft and the Paranormal* (Melrose, Ely, 2005).
Wilson, Ian, *In Search of Ghosts* (Headline Book Publishing Company, London, 1995) 45–46.
Winchester, Alf, 'Why the Spheres Are Invisible – Spirit Photographs', *Noah's Ark*, 4, 57 (April 1995).

Picture Credits

Index

Index

Monsters Caught on Film
Dr Melvyn Willin
ISBN: 978-0-7153-3774-5

From the Loch Ness Monster to the Yeti and Bigfoot, *Monsters Caught on Film* is a thrilling collection of a variety of monster photographs. Each compelling picture is accompanied by illuminating commentary from paranormal expert and psychical investigator, Dr Melvyn Willin. Five chapters cover everything from extinct species and living dinosaurs, to lake monsters, unknown apes and other creatures.

Ghosts Caught on Film 3
Gordon Rutter
ISBN: 978-0-7153-3903-9

An all new compendium of more extraordinary phenomena caught on film. Featuring a selection of contemporary ghost pictures collected as part of a ground-breaking survey by popular psychologist, Richard Wiseman and leading Fortean, Gordon Rutter. Paranormal expert Gordon Rutter explores this intriguing collection which includes shadowy figures, strange mists and ghostly apparitions

Loved this book?
Tell us what you think and you could win another fantastic book from David & Charles in our monthly prize draw.
www.lovethisbook.co.uk

Ghost Chronicles: Stories of the Paranormal
Various
ISBN: 978-0-7153-3779-0

Each of the three books in the set contains around 15 of the very best ghost stories ever told, from the most haunted house in England at Borley Rectory, to the ghosts that roam the Tower of London, and the creepy goings-on aboard the Mary Celeste. Packed with classic tales from yesteryear and more recent ghostly happenings from across the world, *Ghost Chronicles* is the ultimate accessory for any Halloween party or paranormal enthusiast.

The Angels Among Us
Skye Alexander
ISBN: 978-0-7153-3851-3

The amazing appearances of shining lights, winged figures and celestial visions make this uplifting book of photographs a must for anyone interested in angels. Featuring an astounding collection of unexplained images of guardian angels and mysterious spirits, this book is a treat for all fans of angels, apparitions and the occult.

A DAVID & CHARLES BOOK
© F&W Media International, Ltd 2012

David & Charles is an imprint of F&W Media International, Ltd
Brunel House, Forde Close, Newton Abbot, TQ12 4PU, UK

F&W Media International, Ltd is a subsidiary of F+W Media, Inc
10151 Carver Road, Suite #200, Blue Ash, OH 45242, USA

First published in the UK and US as *Paranormal Caught on Film*,
2008, *Ghosts Caught on Film*, 2007 and *Ghosts Caught on Film 2*,
2009

ISBN-13: 978-1-4463-0271-2 paperback
ISBN-10: 1-4463-0271-7 paperback

Printed in China by RR Donnelley for:
F&W Media International, Ltd
Brunel House, Forde Close, Newton Abbot, TQ12 4PU, UK

10 9 8 7 6 5 4 3 2 1

Trade Community Leader: Judith Harvey
Assistant Editor: Hannah Kelly
Art Editor: Sarah Underhill
Production Controller: Kelly Smith

F+W Media publishes high quality books on a wide range of
subjects.
For more great book ideas visit: www.rucraft.co.uk